IT'S SO EASY
WHEN YOU KNOW HOW

"Harry Morgan Moses has done it—he has 'enlightenment' and shows us how to get it. I love his book, It's So Easy When You Know How. Get one, read it and share it with those you truly love."

Mark Victor Hansen, Coauthor of
Chicken Soup for the Soul

"In Harry Morgan Moses' power-packed book, you will learn it is possible to live a life from inspiration rather than desperation, a life lived from high consciousness as well as integration with community and global responsibility. He helps us remember that the the Light shining on our paths is within us all. I like the way he says it."

Mary Manin Morrissey
Author of *Building Your Field of Dreams*

"Moses explores one of life's most important lessons…that the 'world out there' is inseparable from our own consciousness and we have a 'major role to play in our reality.' The sooner we learn this lesson the more joyful and fulfilled our lives will be. Do something constructive for your reality. Read this book!"

Larry Dossey, M.D., Author of *Healing Words, Meaning and Medicine, Recovering the Soul* and *Space, Time & Medicine*

"Harry is an up and coming leader in New Thought. His understanding of science, philosophy and spirituality makes it seem so easy…because he knows how!"

Brian O'Leary Ph.D. Author of *Exploring Inner and Outer Space, Mars 1999 and The Second Coming of Science*

"This book is filled with the wisdom we all need. It will show us how to fulfill our lives with an abundance of everything."

Edith Stauffer, Ph.D. Author of
Unconditional Love & Forgiveness

"This exciting book is definitely a new idea whose time has come…revealed in simple, modern language, it speaks to who and what we really are. At a crucial time when we're in the midst of individual and global transformation, we now have the book that can lead us to where we all want to be for the rest of our lives!"

Dr. Domenic A. Polifrone

*A funny thing
about awareness;
you discover you have it,
then you discover
you had it all along,
you just weren't
aware of it.*

H.M.M.

Library of Congress Cataloging-in-Publication Data:

Moses, Harry Morgan.
  It's So Easy When You Know How / Harry Morgan Moses
1sr ed. p. 158
2nd ed. p. 158
  ISBN: 1-886578-00-1
  $12.00 (pbk)
  1. Psychology 2. Self-directed
  I. Title
BF 632 M67 1995

NTC PRESS

8798 Complex Drive
San Diego, California 92123

www.newthought.org

IT'S SO EASY WHEN YOU KNOW HOW

HARRY MORGAN MOSES

Edited by

Trey Scott

ACKNOWLEDGMENTS

Books are written on years turned inside-out by ideas that never let go until you get them in print.

Richard Bach

Who would have guessed there were so many involved in writing a book…

To the team, I trust we can play again.

To Derinda, you keep feeling, it's what you're good at, your love and support is always felt.

To all those in the field of *Amazing Consciousness*, my love and gratitude, now and always.

The credits will roll at the end of the movie!

When this book was first released there seemed to be a feeling among individuals seeking to help themselves along the path of self awareness that, "Hey, life is not easy!" I never implied nor do I think experience tells us that life, left unattended, is easy.

Life and all the facets of life requires that we pay attention and "wake up" When we become aware of the mechanisms of Mind and learn how to use them our struggles are robbed of hopelessness and indeed, the more we know the easier things get. Yes, it is easy *when* you know how.

Getting the know-how requires dedication and commitment. Yet, with commitment, the rewards are magnificent. Readers from all over the nation and abroad have written to tell me of the deeper joy, the restored relationships and even healings which happened in their lives because they took the time to get some, "know-how."

I'm glad that we've touched lives. I'm glad so many many souls are willing to commit to making their lives easier. After all, we deserve it!

After we sold out of the first edition, this edition of ISE has been edited to make "getting the know-how more accessible. It can be read in sequence or just pick it up and let the simple truths touch your life at random.

I'm glad we found each other, once again.

Highest Love,

Harry Morgan Moses

Del Mar, California

Spring 1999

TABLE OF CONTENTS

Foreword

Back in the early '70s, there was a little nightclub on Melrose in Los Angeles called *The Improvisation*. I had the opportunity to hear a couple of blues players by the name of Sonny Terry and Brownie McGhee. They had been touring the country since the days of the depression. Sonny was blind and Brownie had suffered from Polio at a young age. They wore their courage with an open and profound sense of dignity.

Well into the lively performance, there was a pause and Brownie began to play a solo on his guitar. A hush fell over the crowd as the sweet tones from this well-worn guitar vibrated through the audience. The still in the night club was striking. He played for some time and then looked up at the crowd, and in the silence between the notes said, "It's so easy when you know how."

Brownie had announced a striking and profound life principle. This book is dedicated to the individual in every field who has taken the time to know how and make it easy.

CHAPTER ONE

GRADUATING FROM THE 2 X 4 SCHOOL

Three times and you're in.

The pathway to easy living is grounding ourselves in practices which support us in awakening to the reality that we are spiritual beings. All the intellectual knowledge in the world is insufficient to give us the feeling, the conviction, the deep understanding that this is the absolute Truth. For most of us, this learning has been difficult to come by. We have been bumped and bruised and battered along the course of the way, because we have been unwilling to read the signs which are everywhere present. If you follow the signs, the need to be repeatedly hit on the side of the head with a two by four is transformed to a smooth sail on the eternal oceans of life.

My being became lighter and lighter, I sensed myself moving forward in an upward kind of direction, out toward what was obviously the source of light. I sensed other beings traveling in the same direction, yet unconcerned and in dialogue with the voice that responds to my prayers. I journeyed forward.

"This is an interesting dream" I said.

The voice responded, "Yes, it is interesting."

"It feels very nice here."

The voice responded "Yes, it is nice."

"What am I doing here?"

The voice responded "I just wanted to know why you are so angry?"

"Oh, because I didn't seem to get it exactly the way I wanted it all of the time."

The voice responded, "What did you get?" "I seem to get it the way You wanted it to be most all of the time." The voice responded, "You didn't like what I gave you?"

"No, what you gave me was very nice."

The voice responded, "Much of the time I gave you more than you wanted."

I said "Oh, yes. That's true. But I didn't get it my way."

The voice responded "Didn't you ask me to guide, guard, direct and protect you and lead you into the paths which would reveal and reflect your highest good?"

"Well, yes, I did."

The voice responded "So what's your point?"

I said, "Well, never mind."

I woke up at the bottom of the mountain, aware of my life, aware of my immediate family, and aware of the pain, as I had just fallen 210 feet over a cliff. The rocks, in that moment, seemed more solid than my body.

While the fall was real, and the dialogue was real, the words were changed to make a point. Each of us has a purpose and our anger, our fear, our doubt, our resentments, our untruths and the gap between our intentions and our actions, stand in the way of our fulfillment. That's the hard news. The comforting news is that these things that act as blocks can be transformed into attitudes and habits and practices which place us securely on the path to fulfillment.

As a young child, and throughout my childhood, I had always been happy, I had always been healthy and for the most part, I got my way. For the most part, what I intended to do and the actions that I took, were harmonious.

In the latter part of my teens I became more and more immersed in the patterns of my peers and surrendered my individuality to do the popular thing at the popular time with the popular people. The theme song of my generation was sex, drugs and rock 'n' roll. Fortunately for me, the universe had a better idea and out of the apparent blue, I found myself crippled in the hospital, unable to walk, with a prognosis which was not encouraging.

These things that act as blocks can be transformed into attitudes and habits and practices which place us securely on the path to fulfillment.

I had developed multiple blood clots from my ankle to my hip in my left leg. Beyond the excruciating pain, the medical profession, in its valiant attempt to determine the origin of the disease, nearly killed me by injecting into my system materials to which I had a violent allergic reaction. I was told that while it was possible I would walk again, it would be for short distances with a need to rest and elevate my leg on a regular basis. All hopes of skiing were to be banished from my mind. And what I had known as a healthy responsive body, if I was lucky, would be adequate for survival.

To the happy-go-lucky Harry who had always had his way, this did not seem like good news. After a myriad of tests, the doctors were unable to determine the root of my problem and the best guess was a congenital distortion which could possibly be discovered through exploratory surgery. This was an option which did not seem appealing to healthy-happy-Harry. For the first time in my life, I appeared to be facing a no-win situation.

A 6 foot 5 inch bald-headed gentleman with little round spectacles looking like Ghandi on steroids arrived to dialogue with me about the nature of the Universe.

My brother called me in the hospital and asked if I wanted to speak to a friend of his who was a philosopher and spiritual journeyer. I was willing to talk to anybody about anything, because I was definitely lost. Later that afternoon a 6 foot 5 inch bald-headed gentleman with little round spectacles looking like Ghandi on steroids arrived to dialogue with me about the nature of the Universe. His name was Bill.

Outside of my hospital room was a large billboard which read, TOUGH. In little red letters above the word, "tough" was written the word, "Chevette." Indeed my entire situation felt pretty tough. Well, other than a brief introduction, Bill didn't get a chance to get much of a word in edgewise. For about an hour and a half I explained to him my philosophy of life, my experiences in altered states of consciousness, my belief in past lives.

At the end of the conversation, Bill stood up and said, "Harry there are two things I would like you to know. I'm glad to have met you and everything is going to work out okay." He shook my hand and left the room. As I watched his bald head recede through the little window in the hospital door, I turned to look outside, re-read the billboard which said TOUGH and I started to laugh because I knew that Bill was right. Everything was going to work out okay and everything wasn't tough.

Within 24 hours my blood count returned to normal, the swelling in my leg had been significantly reduced and the team of medical doctors agreed that I could be released from the hospital. Soon after I was restored to health. My skiing was better than ever, my career began to demonstrate greater success and I was on a conscious search for a life partner and family.

I wanted to know what this man knew. He knew that we are spiritual beings having a human experience. Along the course of our relationship he taught me about the power in a new thought and how to use the laws of mind.

Several years later, happily married with an expanding career and expecting a second child, my wife and I were visited by some friends, and we decided to go to the local mountains for a hike. We arrived at the base of a canyon where I looked up the mountain. I decided to climb it simply because it was there. I suggested to my wife and her girlfriend that they stay below with the baby, and my friend and I proceeded up the mountain. About six feet from the crest of the hill, just below the ridge, I spotted a rock. If I put my weight on it, I was sure I could reach the top and pull myself over. The canyon we were climbing was made mostly of granite and indeed, some of that granite was decomposing. Carefully and meticulously, being an experienced hiker, I put my weight on the rock to test its strength. It seemed secure. When I executed the maneuver, the rock gave way under my foot and I began to slide down. Desperately reaching to grab a rock, a plant, a tree, everything crumbled under the force of my weight moving down hill. Within seconds, I realized I was going to be launched over the precipice at which point I screamed, "Oh, my God." My particular version of a near death experience, perhaps better stated, an awakened-to-life experience, didn't involve any particular religious icon but was rather an extension of my re-discovered dialogue with the presence of my own existence, the one that is greater than I am; IS what I am.

Within seconds, I realized I was going to be launched over the precipice at which point I screamed, "Oh, my God."

It is true. I went on a journey of some sort. I left this plane of existence. I was "gone" for about 20 minutes. From my perspective it was an on-going experience of myself in a body different than the one that I presently occupy. Yet I felt very much like me. I never felt anything was wrong. In fact, I thought everything was really quite nice. When I returned to my body and slowly re-awakened to the awareness of what was happening, I was immediately aware that I was okay. I was aware of my wife, my daughter and I knew that the baby in her womb was a boy and that we would all know each other very, very well.

It took a team of advanced surgeons about 5 1/2 hours to sew me back together. Remarkably enough, I didn't break a single bone in my body, nor did I damage any of my internal organs. I used the techniques of affirmation, meditation, positive attitude and spiritual mind treatment to restore my body, so that within a matter of months, I found myself on the ski slopes on a pathway of a more radiant health than I had ever known before.

I was quite confident that my isolated spiritual journey was sufficient for my needs, and I once again returned to work and pursued the successes of this world.

I believe these experiences were trying to show me something, but I didn't know what it was that I was being shown. I was admittedly angry at the universe because I didn't believe that I needed to fall off a mountain to learn that I was a spiritual being, that I would continue to live my life no matter what happened to my physical body. So I had a new kind of anger, and I felt justified in my anger.

I had a mortgage, a recently remodeled house, two kids, two cars, insurance policies, career, beautiful wife, and I was curiously unsatisfied, for no apparent reason. Several years passed and *out of the blue*, I was once again struck with multiple blood clots from my ankle to my hip, this time in the right leg. At 2 AM, when

Infinity cannot deny itself to itself because there is only One.

the pain was more than I could handle, in desperation, I called my friend Bill and shared my dilemma. In his wisdom, he offered a spiritual mind treatment: a simple, definite statement of belief in the spiritual nature of reality, an understanding that in a field of infinite possibilities there is a solution, and if the solution is needed now, it must be available now. Infinity cannot deny itself to itself because there is only One.

In short order, I was checked into the hospital and the doctors once again, began their relentless pursuit to discover the cause of my disease. Their prognosis was once again negative. In fact, a large panel of doctors and experts had arrived at the conclusion that perhaps I was not meant for this plane of existence. I know this because my wife attended the panel meeting and heard the oration of their conclusion. Yet at this point, having been hit by a "two by four" more than once in my life, I knew that I <u>would</u> get better and I knew there was a message for me which I was not hearing or seeing, but I believed was nonetheless present.

The doctor in charge of my case was convinced it was necessary to determine the pathway by which the blood in my leg was following. I warned him of my extreme allergic reaction to the chemical that is used in this procedure. He instructed the physician who was implementing the test to use an alternative material which had been developed in the interim, ten years since I had last had such a procedure. The doctor now in charge of the tests believed it was unnecessary and injected into my system a substance which again, almost killed me. I could feel myself leaving my body which seemed to be the way to move beyond the pain. In that moment, I made a conscious decision to stay. The reaction passed and now it was time to get healed.

As I have mentioned before, the word heal comes from an ancient English word, *haelon,* which means to make whole. It became evident to me that I needed to make all of my life whole. At that point I made a decision to forgo my demands and expectations and do whatever was necessary to comfortably live my life and fulfill my purpose.

Within a year, I had more money, more success, and a greater sense of aliveness than I had ever known before. My skiing had improved, my love for the arts had expanded, and my commitment to humanity and to the earth had become clarified in my experience. It became clear to me that the only purpose which I could follow was *my* purpose, the one that I came here to fulfill. I believe this purpose is like a diamond with multiple facets. Many of the facets are unpolished and therefore lack a certain clarity. Yet, I am aware that the True Self of myself is indeed a precious gem. I have had some success in polishing some of the facets. I believe my purpose is to live in wholeness and inspiration, and I trust that my participation in life will heal, uplift and inspire.

I do not walk the path perfectly, but it is a path that makes my life easier. It brings me rewards that are tangible, and the most valuable part is the deep sense of aliveness which is not tangible, cannot be proven and can only be experienced.

I believe each and every soul, each and every individual has a right to experience this deep sense of aliveness. I believe the planet needs us to wake up to this life so that individually and collectively we can begin to heal ourselves, to return ourselves to wholeness, to return ourselves to aliveness and live in the conscious understanding that God is, I am and it is good!

I know from experience. I've seen it in my own life, and I've seen it in the lives of many, that you can change your mind, get a larger perspective, and positively impact your mental state, your physical health and your environment. I know from experience that when you've finished with the two by fours, what happens to us is a new life, a life of joy, fun, richness, texture, depth, color and adventure.

In the chapters that follow, we strive in the most amiable manner to present the argument that the only thing of real value is true Spiritual conviction.

CHAPTER TWO

THOUGHTS ARE THINGS

*Thoughts are more than things;
they are the cause of things.*

I happen to like this plane of existence. I love to ski. I like roller coasters. I like to play with gravity for fun. I love the beach. I love cars. Disneyland is a car show for me.

These are all things on this plane of existence. Do they have value in and of themselves? Not really. Because everything on this plane of existence came and came to pass. So you are not here to have anything. "You can't take it with you." You can use it all, but you can't keep it.

Things have value if they have value to you. I think that the earth is beautiful. I am into doing Earth. I like the Earth. That's my perception. At a deeper level, I recognize that I am in a timeless reality. I understand the more I can collect the little moments of love, little moments of peace, little moments of providence and little moments of wisdom, the more I can participate in giving back to life and the more expanded my awareness.

Goethe said, "...the most difficult thing is to turn your thoughts into actions." I would challenge that concept and suggest that the most difficult thing is **figuring out what you want**. Not necessarily what you might want in the short term, like material possessions, relationships, sexual experiences, or money, but what you want in the long run.

What is it you really want from life?

Not too long ago, Barbara Walters was questioning Sean Connery about his long and enduring career and all of the roles and the great variety of characters he had played. Paraphrasing Mr. Connery, he suggested he was able to be so many different people because he was quite content being himself.

The only enduring happiness comes from understanding ourselves, seeing ourselves as valuable and being comfortable with who we are.

This book is about long term happiness. It's about understanding ourselves and becoming comfortable in our own body, on this planet, in our universe. This is a state of mind which can be attained regardless of circumstances, conditions, or past experience.

When we know how to live comfortably in our own skin, life becomes easy. The successful individuals throughout history have demonstrated that when things become easy, being productive, being creative, being of service, being successful and having fun is all part of the experience.

Perhaps the starting point for easy living is to take a look at what life is. When you and I are willing to look at ourselves, we don't have to be neurosurgeons

The only enduring happiness comes from understanding ourselves, seeing ourselves as valuable and being comfortable with who we are.

to realize that we did not create the life principle that lives as us. We do not beat our own heart, we do not even breathe our own breath. While you may be able to regulate these things, they are in truth, done unto you. The life that is done unto you existed before you became aware of it, and it stands to reason that it will exist after you leave this plane of existence called Planet Earth.

Since something is being done unto you and you didn't create it, you must be part of or related to, that which does the doing. The understanding of this relationship between the Life that moves in you and you, is the starting point for easy living.

This mechanism of life, by the authority of its being, seems to be able to "do." By the very act of reading this book, you are demonstrating that you have the power to make choices and to act upon them. So it would appear that the ability to, "be" and to, "do" is recreated in you. As we look more deeply into this concept, we will discover that it is the mechanism of choice that is the starting point for all activity. The level of our confidence in our ability to make a choice and the conviction in the choice we make, seems to dictate the degree of impact our decisions may have on our own lives or the lives of others.

Live your life embracing, accepting and honoring everything that you are right here and right now. This means honoring yourself as a human being.

It is the artist who believes that he can paint that creates the painting. It is the inventor who is sure that the answer exists that creates the invention. It is the business person most convinced of his own ability to make a deal that makes the biggest deal. So self-confidence is a key to easy living. The question is, how do I get self-confidence?

It is easy to simply say that in order to have self-confidence, you have to know who you are. In order to know who you are, you have to know what you are and your relationship to the whole. To live successfully, you must have confidence in the Whole, or Life, or the Universe or Ralph, (as Dr. Wayne Dyer suggests is a perfectly good name). The highest respect you can pay your Creator is to live your life and live it well. Live your life embracing, accepting and honoring everything that you are right here and right now. This means honoring yourself as a human being.

Easy living is about knowing. Its about knowing a Truth that is self-existent and does not need your approval nor your belief in It in order to exist. Yet to become valuable and pertinent to you, you must know It.

> *The Cosmos would be fairly chaotic if laws could not operate without the sanction of human belief.*
> Yogananda

No doubt you've heard, "And you shall know the truth, and the truth shall make you free." The interesting thing about this statement is that it does not say the Truth shall make you free. Knowing the Truth makes you free. The only place you can know something is in your conscious mind. In order to have awareness, you must be conscious of it or it isn't a real awareness. The spirit of awareness is found in your conscious mind. Repositioning our understanding of the importance of our conscious mind and its relationship to the whole can be a challenging concept. The

Spirit of your own existence is found in your conscious mind.

Doesn't this throw a cog in the wheel for those of us who are even slightly aware of the concepts in psychology? The general understanding in psychology suggests that the greatest part of your mind is what is called the subconscious mind. Not only is it the greatest part of your mind, but it is what holds the seat of all of your memory. So everything you have ever known, said or done is held within your subconscious mind.

The journey of expanding our confidence is about expanding our awareness of Life principles and understanding how to use them.

Now, we are suggesting that the only power there is in creation, is self consciousness, and we must be aware in order to have power. So the psychologist may say, "Well, that's a bunch of hooey, because I already know that the subconscious mind is much bigger than the conscious mind." But there's an interesting thing about awareness, if you have it and you are not conscious of it, you are totally unaware. You see, awareness without a conscious awareness, is not awareness at all.

Common sense is not common practice.

Aren't there some things in your world that you just know? "I just know," and there's no argument to that thing. Because there is no argument to that thing, it shows up as working in your life. This kind of conviction has been described through the ages as faith. The philosopher Ernest Holmes describes faith as an attitude so convinced of itself that it knows no opposites. This attitude of conviction, this confidence, or this faith, exists within each of us in different levels. We have faith in ourselves, faith in someone, and faith in many things. Faith or conviction in the Spirit, the Universe, God, Creator or Ralph (It does not care what you call It), is an attitude necessary for easy living.

Wouldn't it be nice if we could move from a place of wishing, to knowing there is a Power and a presence and a life force that is in us and among us, that is with us and for us, that cannot be denied. Wouldn't it be nice to really know that?

The journey of expanding our confidence is about expanding our awareness of Life principles and understanding how to use them.

AIKIDO

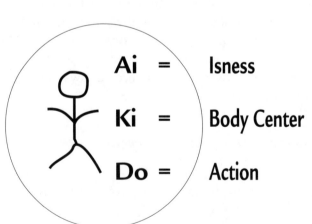

The Japanese martial art Aikido makes reference to different aspects of our being: "Ai"-means isness, "ki"-the center of your solar plexus, "do"-doing. The art comes from bringing "Ai," the energy of the Universe into our experience, into our body, "ki" and letting it do, "do." You and I are so busy doing, without the energy of the Universe ("Ai"), that we wonder how come our lives are filled with struggle. How come we can't really seem to make things happen? The reality is that you and I do not create the Power, you and I use the Power. You and I are the place where we can allow that Power to operate. We allow that power to operate by making choices.

Our thoughts are not creative, they merely use a creativity.

Ernest Holmes

The clearer the choice, the greater the confidence, the faster the *demonstration*. The dictionary defines the word demonstration as, *to prove by making real.* We are interested in proving—by demonstrating lives well-lived—that it is easier to *use* the power of choice, to cooperate with the

Life is more than going, getting and having.

mechanisms of nature, than it is to try to create the power. Attempting to create the power leads to inevitable failure. **Using** the power leads to personal empowerment.

The process of decision is knowing what you want, deciding you shall have it and acting upon it. As we look more closely, we may discover that what we really want is to live our lives well, to be comfortable in our own body and to have a deep-seated confidence in the nature of the universe.

It's up to each one of us to take the grand step and perceive things more clearly.

I can learn to cooperate with the nature of evolution. I can learn to cooperate with the laws of consciousness and expand my awareness. Roy Eugene Davis, a modern metaphysical teacher says, "Right action is continually being willing to grow."

Life is more than going, getting and having. Life is about experiencing time in the only moment there is, NOW. Dr. Jean Houston, the cultural anthropologist says, "We should always be in a state of receptivity to an omnipresent gift rather than yearning for the attainment of some distant goal."

For too long, we have put our attention on our misunderstanding and misinterpretation of religion and time. What does religion teach about time? Most all religions basically teach a timeless nature and they teach the importance of living in the *Religion is not God, it is a bridge to God.* here and now, being present in *this* moment. What has happened is we have gotten into the religious version of things and put our attention on the religion instead of the essence. Religion itself is the bridge to the experience of God, not God. As a civilized race, we have put our attention on religion, focused all our energy on the bridge, so much so that through our warring and hatred, we extracted a great deal of "civilized" out of civilization. The bridge was only something we were supposed to cross to get to the experience. Time is not life, time is how we experience life. Religion is not God, it is a bridge to God.

The soul is not something we should connect with when we die but is the thread of continuity between all lives. Your soul, the idea of your individuality in the mind of God, exists for you now and bridges one life to the next.

The only life you can ever know is the life you are in contact with NOW. The only thing you will ever understand is that which you tell yourself in a language that makes sense to you.

If you are waiting for sufficient scientific evidence to show up to support your conviction to participate in life, you may be waiting a very long time. Scientific evidence will not give you conviction. Would that it could. You could read the literature that is found in virtually any modern self-help section and you'd be free. There is more than enough evidence to verify a relationship between consciousness and experience, but evidence is not enough.

Conviction must be born from the inside. In order to live the life of your dreams, easily, comfortably, creatively, YOU are going to have to be willing to perceive an expanded reality and the starting point for this expansion is a new thought.

CHAPTER THREE

ATTITUDES IN ACTION

*To use the creative process you must
discover the creative process.*

In order to live easily we have to have
certain basic understandings. The essential nature of easy
living is that you are now, the sum total of everything you
have ever thought, said, or done. Since you cannot say anything, or do anything, without first thinking (admittedly,
many things are done without a great deal of thought), it is
fair to say that your mind creates your experience. Whatever experience you may have had or may be having—
good, bad or indifferent—these experiences are based on
thoughts and ideas and attitudes which are creating the experience of your life. If your experiences are bad, these experiences are based on thoughts and ideas and attitudes
which are working against you toward the fulfillment of
your life.

You are not bad, or a sinner for having thoughts and attitudes and guilts that are working against you. There's not
much difference between New Age guilt, Catholic guilt,
Jewish guilt, Mama's guilt, or any other kind of guilt. Guilt
is guilt and it works against you!

Where did these negative attitudes come from?

Attitudes are filters through which we view the world. They
operate the same way as a pair of sun glasses. When you are
wearing the sunglasses, you see the world through those

hues and tints. Attitudes are created through learned responses. For example, you might find the optimistic person looking at a cloudy day and proclaiming "What a great day for reading, drawing, walking and taking care of myself." While another person looking at exactly the same day might say, "This is the kind of day that makes you want to roll over and die." Is the day different, or is it simply different in the mind of the perceiver? It is the habit patterns of mind and the assumptions we have made from our past experiences that create our attitudes.

A lot of the negative conditioning we have, we learned from our parents or primary caregivers. As small children, we were told that if we didn't eat what was on our plate, children in Africa would starve. We were told that life's a bitch and then you die. We were told money doesn't grow on trees. We were told to learn the value of a dollar. In addition to all of this, we made a lot of incorrect assumptions as children that have operated in our lives essentially as laws.

Here's a little story. When I was in eighth grade, we had math and science in one room and history and English in another. Between periods, we were required to change classrooms. As normal, healthy eighth graders will tend to be, I was involved in some raucous behavior while changing class rooms: off-color stories, laughing, innuendoes, all that sort of thing. The teacher decided that I was the source of all the com-

Guilt is guilt and it works against you!

motion. He came over to my desk, laid his palms down on each corner, put his nose to my nose, the blood was running to the small capillaries in his face and in the pink of fury, he yelled the question, "Do you think you're somebody special?" I paused for a moment, absorbing the rather peculiar visual which was in my face and I answered the question naturally and calmly, "Yes!"

While it may have sounded like a rude and belligerent response, that was not my intention. My being special in no way inferred that everyone else was not special. Evidently, the inner meaning of my communication was understood. For his response was simply, "Oh." Everyone became calm and class continued.

Had an event of that nature occurred just a year or two earlier, I would have answered "No, I'm not special." I could have easily functioned with this incorrect assumption for the rest of my life. The result of this kind of belief would have operated in my life as a self-imposed law that refused to allow anything more than average to be demonstrated in my experience. By operating on incorrect assumptions, we have tied ourselves to the ordinary.

As small children, there are many opportunities to make incorrect assumptions and therefore operate out of a false premise. Often times in divorced families, children believe they were the cause of the divorce. In bad relationships, children believe the problem in the relationship is their fault. If there are money

I am an adult now, and I am responsible for my own attitudes.

problems in a family, a child, while growing up, can assume that he or she is a burden and not a blessing. These are the kind of childhood assumptions which from an adult point of view, we see as totally false. A child can assume these as real. We may be functioning with childlike assumptions and childlike attitudes in our adult life.

The reality is, that for the orange farmer in Florida, money does grow on trees. The *value* of the dollar in 1956 has very little relationship to the *value* of the dollar today. The inadequate food distribution systems have nothing to do with the food that's on my plate. The truth is, life's a joy and it is eternal.

We picked up a bunch of false ideas along the way. Many of them were taught to us by friends and family and teachers who didn't know any better. I am an adult now, and I am responsible for my own attitudes.

The premise is that my mind creates my experience, my thoughts create my attitudes. It is true on some level that this receptive nature of mind is receiving every thought I think and, in essence, I am constantly giving instruction to this creative capacity. I am at the helm of my destiny…

CHAPTER FOUR

CONSCIOUSNESS

*The essential nature of easy living is that you are
now the sum total of everything you have ever
thought, said and done.*

It is true that you are the sum total of everything you have ever thought, said and done. There is also something within you that projects the ability to think, to speak and to act. This something, combined with your thoughts, feelings and actions, is your total consciousness. It is who and what you are as an individual in the Universe.

The Universe is a whole system. It is the cause of creation. It is that which creates and it is that which is created. As you and I find ourselves in the Universe, we must be part of the system which we call the Universe. Since it exists as that which is in front of form and it exists as that which is behind form, we could conclude that its nature is not form, but is something non-material, perhaps we could call it Spirit.

I am a consciousness within a spiritual system.

My personal consciousness is my capacity to participate with life. Imagine a large, vast and magnificent waterfall. Imagine yourself as very thirsty approaching it. In front of you are containers of various sizes beginning with thimbles, and moving up to a large tub. The size of the container that you choose to drink of the waters of life, represents the amount of consciousness that you currently embody. Do I present a thimble? Do I present a cup? Or do I present a bucket? Regardless how much I draw from the fountain of life, the eternal wellspring will continue to pour out supply, forever! Expanding my capacity to drink in the waters of life is the journey of expanding consciousness.

What are the ways in an organized system for me to expand? How do I know it is an organized system?

There are a lot of different theories about the nature of the Universe. The most common of which is the theory of the

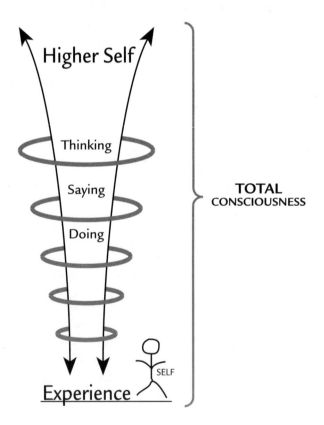

big bang. Interestingly enough, there is no conflict between the story of creation as presented in the Old Testament, in the book of Genesis, and our most contemporary theory of the big bang.

God looked throughout all of the Universe and said, "This is cool."

As we have stated throughout, the primary intelligence of the Universe exists in and through all creation, and in the potential of all creation. So, let me invite your indulgence as we tell a little story.

In the beginning, before anything was, God was being. All of a sudden, it dawned upon the awareness of the Creator that It existed, that It was conscious of Its existence. This posed a dilemma. For It was conscious of Itself and It had nothing to be conscious of. You should have heard the noise. For at that moment, God took a breath and the manifest Universe existed. As all of these gasses and lights and substances were colliding and interacting, it was the kind of color show that the flower children of the late '60s would have truly enjoyed.

As God was watching all of this unfold through the action of Its thought, God looked throughout all of the Universe and said, "This is cool."

Have you ever experienced something that was meaningful, beautiful, or important? Did you look to find the eyes of someone with whom you could share the experience? If you couldn't find such eyes, did you experience an emptiness or a void? What did you do with that emptiness? You sought to fill it.

The Universe abhors a vacuum.

Back to our story…

As God was noticing the magnificence of Its own creation, It sought to share in the magnificence of this creation and there was nobody there. For God was everything and all things. At that moment there was a vacuum. The Universe abhors a vacuum. God filled it with a thought, "I'll have children, the children will grow and discover their relationship with me and I will be able to share the joy of my creation with my creation."

At the point of this thought, the Universe involved everything necessary to evolve a self-conscious individual. At the point of self-consciousness, the creative process begins all over again at the level of the microcosm, or the self-conscious individual.

So it would appear from our little story, that the Universe created you out of Itself in order that it could discover Itself in a new starting point: YOU! At the point of your self-recognition, God, the Universe, or Ralph, shares everything in creation with you. All of this started because the Universe was conscious of Itself, loved Itself and expressed Itself.

That which is the motivating force, or the impulsion for everything is love.

Love never dies, it changes form. We know scientifically, energy never dies. If love is the very impulse of the Universe, if God were sitting there being God and said, "Gosh, it would be nice if there were a place where I could discover myself," then God would need you and me to do that. The levels of intelli-

Expanding my capacity to drink in the waters of life is the journey of expanding consciousness.

gence below self-consciousness are not equipped to identify themselves as involved and therefore an intricate part of creation. The rock is not going to wake up some day and say, "Oh, I am a rock, I am of God." You and I are able to do that. This is what evolution is. Evolution is the out-

Love never dies, it changes form.

pushing of Spirit into that which is already involved. That which is involved from the place of absolute Intelligence evolves.

The life force at the center of our own nature is infused within the nature of God. The ideas involved in the mind of God are not subject to time. Spirit is that which is before time, which is eternity.

> *Eternity is that which is prior to time and eternity must be manifest, therefore, time is necessary.*
> Ernest Holmes

So eternity is something that exists without time, or coexists with time. Spirit measures Itself out through time, which is a sequence of events. And Spirit measures Itself through manifestation. Eternity exists in and of Itself. It doesn't need time to exist, but in order for eternity to express, it has created sequence. Time exists just to keep everything from happening at once.

We have decided that the thing that we use to measure experience, is the experience. For example, you say "Once in my life, I went to a great outdoor music concert in Big Sur." The event has passed, but the memory is real. Remembering is not subject to time. Reality is not subject to time. Psychology tells us that the mind does not know the difference between a perceived reality and reality. The challenge, or opportunity, is expanding our perception of reality. As we've mentioned before, if all life is poured upon you, all the joys of life at any given time, how much of life could you actually accept? Only as much as your consciousness is able to embody.

We have a mind that always responds mathematically, mechanically, perfectly in accord with exactly the perception we give it. When we only make room for a little bit of perception, then that's how much we have in our experience. What do you perceive about life? When will you see that your right to set the laws of creation in motion is already given to you, already poured upon you awaiting your acceptance and use of it?

> *Truth is within ourselves. There is an in-most center in us all, where the Truth abides in fullness; and to know rather consists in opening out a way whence the imprisoned splendor may escape in than effecting entry for a light supposed to be without.*
> Robert Browning

In order to have understanding, you must be conscious. The teaching of empowerment, or easy living, suggests that I have the power to live my life the way I choose to live it. Telling me that I'm a spiritual being, that I am one with the flower, and one with all the cosmos, therefore, I am okay, does not make me okay.

Henry Miller, the author, said, "Don't go around making everything so profound." Let's understand that if your life has been difficult, and you want it to be easy, you are going to have to change. You will not change if you are in an unchangeable mode. You cannot learn if you are convinced that you already know. You cannot stay the same and be transformed.

I'm not trying to give some power to a book, not trying to give some power to any one philosophy. I'm not trying to get you to join in any church, temple, mosque, synagogue, chapel, community or organization. I am suggesting that you are already equipped to give power to yourself.

The phenomenon of consciousness is something very important. The deeper you inquire, you begin to realize it is not only very important but it also seems to be the only thing that is important. It can be difficult for us to accept the idea that my perception determines my reality. Sometimes we wonder, is my perception really enough? This is where we begin to live between two worlds: the world of perception, self-esteem and self-realization, the comfort of the words, "I can do it," and the practical reality of my bills, my pains, my longings and my unfulfilled desires.

You cannot learn if you are convinced that you already know.

The goal is to be transformed, to go beyond the words, beyond the icons, beyond the stuff, to actually hear the voice within yourself say, "I am the power and it lives within me."

You might have heard the story about the two shoe salesmen, who went to the Far East to open up new territories. After three days, the first salesman sent a cablegram to the home office, "Taking next plane back, no prospects here, everyone goes barefoot." After seven days, an envelope arrived at the home office from the second salesman, with a note which read, "Enclosed 50 orders, prospects unlimited, nobody here has shoes!!!"

My attitude can create my experience. My perception of possibilities determines my possibilities. This means how much life I shall

My perception of possibilities determines my possibilities.

have, how much joy I shall have, how much laughter I shall have, how much success I shall have, is determined by my own perception. In short, I establish the criteria. You will find throughout history that successful individuals have been able to think a big thought and to perceive a big idea. The things that seem impossible only became possible because someone perceived the possibility.

> *Only those who will risk going too far can possibly find out how far they can go.*
>   T.S. Elliot

You and I need to dream the big dream. We need to think the big thoughts. We need to understand that we are determining the parameters of our own success. It seems almost impractical to believe that my thoughts and attitudes, dreams and perceptions, are affecting the experience of my life. How does the world know my inner thinking? I have to go about the business of getting up, going to work, taking care of the responsibilities in my life: shopping, drinking, eating, bathing. My inner-most thoughts, my deepseated dreams, my longed-for ambitions are hidden within me and the world doesn't know. Or so it seems.

The truth is that the mechanism of life, with or without your approval, with or without your conscious knowledge, is receiving the impress of your thought and acting upon it. You are immersed in and surrounded by a creative intelligence which is responsive. This means that as far as the universe is concerned, your secret inner life is not so secret. In order to change, in order to live easily, we've got to give something up. We have to surrender the idea that we are separate and isolated.

> *It is not the surrender of that which is happy, it is not a surrender of that which is joyful, it is the surrender of that which has dulled our senses, clouded our vision, dimmed our memory, stifled our imagination.*
>
> Ernest Holmes

For most of us, understanding the mechanism of life means a complete reworking of our understanding of the nature of the Universe. We feel that addressing the issues of the nature of life are things that should be left to the philosophers and the authors of self-improvement books.

Nothing could be further from the truth. We should not go around with a nonchalant attitude of whether we think life is good, or life is mediocre or in-between. As each individual is determining the criteria of their own experience, it becomes essential to become passionate about the reality that life is good. We have to establish within the deepest levels of our own existence the expectancy of good. We need to expect good things to happen. We need to have an attitude so convinced of the goodness of life, that we can maintain our sense of

We have to surrender the idea that we are separate and isolated.

cool in the face of any challenge. Easy living does not mean that we are not required to pay attention. It doesn't mean there aren't going to be situations and circumstances that require a great deal of compassion and a great deal of understanding. We think tenacity, compassion and understanding are

> *Easy living does not mean that we are not required to pay attention.*

things that are hard. They are not hard, but they do require a slight amount of effort. It does require some building to establish a confidence in life. It requires demanding of life that it reveal confidence to you, in you, as you and through you.

All of this is suggesting that you can change your mind and change your experience. Change your mind so that you can change your experience means that **you** have to change your mind. You have to do **your** work.

You need to be passionate about the realization, about experiencing for yourself the reality that life is good. But, you need to be detached in the way that it happens. We can understand that our attachment to the way things happen and our belief that it isn't happening the way that we want it oftentimes limits or restricts us. Our limited parameters don't enable us to experience life coming to us in new and more wonderful ways because we have established a limited criteria. But, life can come to you in new, exciting, unexpected ways. Meister Eckhart, the 15th century mystic said, "Divinity is not old and tired and controlling and judgmental, but spontaneous, playful, erotic and full of surprises."

Somehow we've come up with the idea in our society, that we should get progressively more by doing progressively less. The truth is, you get progressively more by progressively becoming something more. Things then start to show up in your world as a logical progression from your inner growth to your outer experience. It is true that you can appear to be doing a lot less. A day's work for a day's pay is an old concept. You cannot become truly prosperous if you have to be physically present to earn your good. Yet, in order to learn how to create passive income, you must be actively involved in your personal growth and development.

Perhaps you've heard the story of the factory that broke down. This factory runs at $70,000 a minute. Every minute it shuts down it's losing money. In desperation, the manager of the factory calls the repair guy. The guy comes up to fix the factory. He walks around the factory for a little while, looks around, sees a spot and takes out a screw. He reaches into his pocket, he puts in a new screw, turns the switch on and the factory is running again. The boss is so grateful, he says, "This is wonderful, this is fabulous, how much do I owe you?" The repair man says "$10,000." The boss says "$10,000!!? You were here for a minute and a half, I demand an invoice." The repair man draws up an invoice and hands it to the boss and it says, *one screw: .05. $9,999.95 for knowing where to put it.*

Increasing your understanding, is how we get more.

KNOW-HOW SERVICES, INC.

ITEM	PRICE
#6 Screw	0.05
Know-how	9999.95
TOTAL	$10,000.00

Increasing our understanding, is how we get more. The more we get on the inside, the more we build our consciousness, the easier things get in our experience because we have worked on building something on the inside that is reflected on the outside. That which is on the inside is invisible. Consciousness is invisible.

Things which are seen are not made of things which do appear.

Hebrews 11:3

Everything which exists is created twice. First, there is the idea, then there is the form. The clearer the idea, the better the form. For example, if you attempt to build a house without the proper plans, your idea is not clear. Therefore, you will have to fix the mistakes along the way, and the house will cost you more than a house built with a well-thought out and well-executed plan. Both the house built without a plan and the house built with the plan are created more than once, because there has got to be an idea before there is form. Clear ideas are built by thought. Ideas repeated, create attitudes, attitudes create our experience. We are interested in this invisible world of creation, the world of thought which is the world which molds our experience.

Everything which exists is created twice.

If we break down the term metaphysics, we find the Greek word, *meta*, which can mean in front of, along with, or beside. The second part of the word, *physics*, implies that which is physical. Easy living is about creating easy lives *in front of the form*. The more optimistic our attitudes, the easier our lives. Doing the work, creating the thoughts, establishing the ideas, repeating the ideas, building the attitudes is a responsibility which must be assumed by each one of us.

If you and I had the same faith as an electrician, we would be better metaphysicians.

Ernest Holmes

We understand there are laws and principles that work from what we call the invisible into that which is visible. Not too complicated right? There are invisible laws and principles from which everything comes. There is no thing in the physical world that exists without an idea behind it. Apparently there is some system in the universe, some organic natural structure in the universe that can move the idea into form. There may be a process involved, but there is a system that causes ideas to move into form. The greater the enthusiasm, the deeper the belief, the more profound the motivation, the faster it happens. So enthusiasm, motivation and belief act as a law. There is a law of mind that causes things to happen. It operates at the level of belief.

When an electrician wires things together to operate a light, he sets them up in cooperation with the laws of electricity. He turns the switch and expects the light to go on. If it doesn't go on, he knows there's something wrong with the wiring and he fixes it.

In our lives, we are operating a mental law. It is acting on the total of our beliefs and creating our experience. If you and I had confidence in the universe,

There is a law of mind that causes things to happen. It operates at the level of belief.

and confidence in the law of the universe, we would look at our world when 'the light doesn't go on' and we would know that we've screwed up the wiring somewhere. We would go about the business of repairing the circuitry that did not cooperate with the natural law of the Universe.

If I'm in relationship, and the light doesn't go on, I'm not relating the right way. If I'm in financial issues, and the light doesn't go on, I am not functioning with a healthy, prosperous attitude. If I am in health issues and the light doesn't go on, I'm not understanding the structures of my own health.

Fixing the wiring requires confidence in the structures of the Universe and a dependency on natural laws.

This planet spins at exactly the right speed to cause gravity to be a consistent law. It spins around the sun, so as to make a complete journey approximately every 365 days. The relationship between the planet and the sun remains intact. The relationship between this solar system and this galaxy and an ever-expanding universe is held in a perfect order. On this plane of existence, water seeks its own level in accord with its own weight. Supplies of fresh water are constantly recirculated. Electricity can be used in accord with laws of resistance to make possible extraordinary technologies. The acorn knows how to become an oak tree. The instincts within the animals seem to be able to cause them to be able to survive and recreate their species. The tadpole is going to become a frog.

Everywhere we look, we see intelligence. The truth is, we live in an intelligent universe which operates intelligently. Evolution moves in a progression, starting with the intelligence we find within the plant and the mineral. It evolves to the simple consciousness in the animal that can think, but cannot think about what it thinks about. Then it moves to the self-conscious individual.

We live in an intelligent universe which operates intelligently.

I think, therefore I am.

Descartes

Progressing upward it arrives at the liberating level of consciousness which can think about its relationship to the whole. Self-realization leads to what is called Cosmic Consciousness.

What we find lacking in the human condition is any apparent pre-programming. Because at the point of self consciousness, evolution ceases to be automatic. This means all hope of advancing faster than a law of averages rests on the individual's decision to recognize, understand and use the creative forces in the universe. You and I make this decision by using the mechanism of our will, which is that part of us which is able to make and maintain choices.

You can make the choice to build your consciousness and expand your awareness. Expanding your awareness, building your consciousness, is the pathway to easy living.

CHAPTER FIVE

The Will

The Truth is, we live in an intelligent Universe which operates intelligently.

The easiest way to use the creative process is to deepen our understanding of the nature of the Universe. In Western traditions, we have chosen certain books which represent our sacred literature. It is fair to say that the Old Testament qualifies as one of those sacred books. The first book of the Old Testament is the book of Genesis. The poets who wrote that book describe the creative process in a very palatable manner. God said, "Let there be," and there was.

This simple phrase announces the triune nature of the universe, or three different aspects of the One life which recreates Itself in each of us.

God said, "Let there be." If God is going to say anything, or if you and I are going to say anything, we must be conscious in order to say it. So we recognize that one of the qualities of the Universe is the quality of being conscious. If there is only one Universe, *Uni* meaning one, *verse* meaning song, then when God said, God must have said something to something. But since there is only one thing, God said something to Itself. God said, "Let there be." The result of God saying "Let there be" is form…the physical Universe as we know it.

The short form is whatever God says, **IS**. The thing spoken, the thing spoken to, the creative result of that action, are all aspects of one process:

The Creative Process

You and I are born in and function as a living part of the creative process. The creative process begins in each one of us, with the conscious act of saying, "Let there be." While we are living in a world which is waking up to various levels of transcendental realities, for the most part, our culture is unaware of the power of the creative process. There are ideas we have created which we do not want to experience. This is a result of our culture being asleep to the idea that through our conscious mind **every** thought we think is setting the creative process in motion.

> *...the whole country is not in flames, everything going on in America is not represented by those big black headlines on page one.*
>
> Charles Kurault

The aspect of our being which receives the impress of our thought is automatically creative. It has no ability to question or value the creative causes which are set in motion, either by an individual or by society as a whole. We understand that the process of easy living cannot begin in society as a whole; it must begin within the individual consciousness of each individual who seeks to be liberated. If we were to think of society as represented

The creative process begins in each one of us, with the conscious act of saying 'Let there be'.

by a huge sailing vessel, we could understand that someone in the ship must issue the command to the helm. The helm will then execute the action and, very slowly, the large vessel will begin to respond to the changed direction. You and I must assume our rightful positions as captains of the ship and issue a new command, away from the storms and into calm waters.

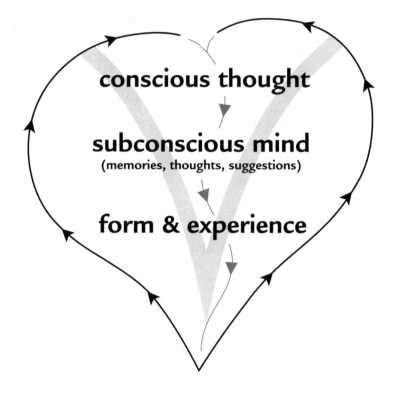

conscious thought

subconscious mind
(memories, thoughts, suggestions)

form & experience

The question we should ask ourselves is where does the creative process begin within me? Each individual is equipped with two facets of their mind: one facet is the conscious mind, the other is the subconscious mind. The subconscious mind receives the impress of your thought, and, at some level, it remembers every thought that it is given. The subconscious mind is not only actively receiving today's thoughts, but it is acting on all of the memories, suggestions, thoughts and ideas which it was given yesterday, and which it has been given throughout our lives. This aspect of ourselves not only has the ability to store memories, it has the ability to create. The thoughts and ideas which we have believed in return in our experience.

Somewhere back in the creative process, God, or Spirit, or Ralph, was going about the business of being.

How does it know how to do that? There is not a scholar or an expert in any field who could tell you how it creates. What we know is that it does, in fact, create.

When we honestly assess ourselves, we can see that we have created belief systems which may not be supporting us in our total well being.

Since the subconscious mind acts as neutral, unable to evaluate the information it is given, we can begin to see that the subconscious mind is subject to information which is processed through the conscious mind. Since this aspect of our mind is creative, and since it knows how to create, to refer to it as less than conscious is not entirely accurate. The subconscious mind always operates in accord with the information given. Therefore, we don't find it less conscious than any other aspect of mind, we find it subject to conscious mind. So perhaps the more accurate term is subjective mind.

There is a creative process within each of us which is responding to the total thought processed through our conscious mind.

In our time, individuals by the thousands are revealing through the course of their personal development this simple understanding. What I think about, comes about.

Since I am free to operate my mind according to my own choices, the mechanism of the will becomes our most powerful tool. The will is the mechanism within the mind that enables us to establish goals and maintain direction. The creative process is what does the work, responding to the choices of the individual. This leads us to understand that it is not so much that our thought is creative; it is that our thought uses a creativity.

Let us be clear. We are not talking about will power. We are talking about using the mechanism of the will to make choices which set the creative process in motion in accord with our personally established goals.

Liberty is not license. The Universe that we live in is self-governing and self-protecting. The fundamental law of its own nature is harmony. This must be so, for if there were not a primary law of harmony, there would be a force acting against it, therefore, the eternal could be destroyed which would make it something less than eternal.

Simply discovering the mechanism of free will, does not in and of itself set us free. For we need to understand that the will operates on several different levels, most easily described as God's will, the will of my Highest Self, and my personal will.

As we make the effort to lift our awareness from the personal to the transpersonal to the cosmic, our consciousness becomes expanded. We reveal greater freedom and easier living.

Doesn't that sound great? Well, what does it mean? Somewhere back in the creative process, God, or Spirit, or Ralph, was going about the business of being. It was all It needed to express Its Beingness, except for the awareness of the consciousness of Itself. So this original life force took a breath (or a bang), and the manifest world was created. Whatever the original life force is, it is conscious of Itself. As It set all creation in motion, It follows that contained within It, is everything necessary to create. Out of that self-existence, everything is created.

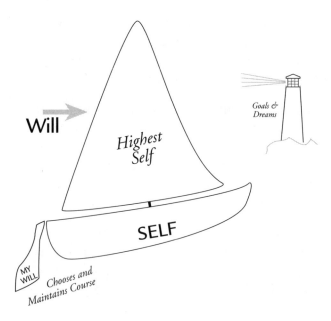

The will of God is to create. That creative force is operating on both the universal and the individual level. Since we are not involved in creating planets and galaxies, we must assume that our personal will, while no doubt connected with all of that process, is not directly involved in that process. Yet the conscious self-expansion of the Universe is something that the will of the Universe is involved in.

It seems to be an ongoing choice of the Universe that it expands and discovers itself. Within that process of evolution (evolution being the result of that creative process which the original intelligence engaged) self-consciousness is born. You possess the consciousness of yourself. You also possess the mechanism of will. Yet on the personal level, the will is capable of making choices which do not harmonize with the intention of the Universe to know itself to coexist with itself, and the original creative impulse of that first breath, which was born out of Spirit's love for Itself.

The will for you, and every human being, exists in two levels. The will of the personal self and the will of your Highest Self, which always knows what to do and how to do it, which always makes choices that are in harmony with the original intention of the Universe. Behind the form of your existence is the idea of your existence. That idea, planted in the womb of Spirit, gives birth to your form. Ideas cannot be destroyed, harmed or diminished. They are always whole and complete. The Divine Idea of your existence (your soul nature) is eternal. Therefore it always make choices which harmonize with all that is eternal.

In our culture in this time, we tend to function out of the personal will with very little regard to any invisible forces which are able to make life more harmonious, richer, fuller, more creative and more prosperous.

Somewhere along the line, we came to believe that surrendering our personal will to any invisible agency was nothing short of religious fervor, or personal irresponsibility. Yet it is clear, in the course of human evolution, that without a radical re-prioritizing, the problems of appalling injustice, wars, famine, disease and malaise will take centuries, if not millenniums, to fix. In the Old Testament it says, "God made man upright and man sought out many inventions." We have quite an imagination haven't we?

Yet, if we are willing to explore the possibilities of an existent energy in the Universe, functioning individually and specifically for each one of us, the possibilities of a revealed synchronicity are unimaginable to even the most enlightened intellectual mind.

Each one of us possess a high level of intelligence. Sometimes called, "transpersonal," sometimes called, "Higher Self," in various religious traditions it is called by different names; Atman, Buddha, Christ-Self, Naphtha, or even Ralph. What we name It is, of course, not important. Learning to access It and discovering methods through which we can rely on It are very important.

The lowest level of will, the will of the personal self, needs to be repositioned so that it really is only involved in making the choice to listen to the Highest Self.

The life of discovering, contacting and revealing the Highest Self is the life of easy living.

Once you get tuned into the awakened life, success and performance and achievement matter less and less…yet they show up more and more.

Wayne Dyer

CHAPTER SIX

HABIT

The mind has an interesting habit; it
acquires habits by the repetition of thought.

There is a mechanism which can set us
on course to tuning in and living in touch with our true
Self. It is a mechanism that you have been using from the
time you were born. As with most natural gifts, most of us
have been using it while we're asleep, thinking that we're
awake. It is the mechanism of habit.

There isn't a soul living who doesn't have a habit. Habits
can be good. Habits can be bad. Habits can be destructive,
and habits can be constructive. We are aware of some of our
habits, and others, we are not. The important thing about
habits is understanding that once we have them, we do
things, for the most part, automatically in accord with the
habit.

There are very few people who drive a car who actually
think about the mechanics of the accelerator, the clutch, the
turn indicators, the mirrors, the windows, the circulating
system, let alone the mechanical processes involved in making all of these things work. Yet, in any major city in the
world there is a huge percentage of drivers arriving at their
destinations. After we have acquired the skills for driving,
we practice them, we acquire habits, and driving is a natural phenomenon.

If you've ever watched an athlete, the millions of reactions and judgments and adjustments necessary in the simple game of tennis, in a casual game of catch, a quick dip in the water, a jog around the track, are too numerable to mention. Yet for the tennis player, the ball player, the swimmer and the runner, its all perfectly natural because they have acquired the habit.

Let us look at how we made these complicated things seem so easy. Each habit starts with a thought. The thought, moved upon, creates an action. We think about the thought and repeat the action, and the process goes on until, at some point, it reaches this invisible place called habit. Habits can be acquired. Habits can be changed, and habits can be dropped. The process of losing a habit, acquiring a habit, or changing a habit is all the same process.

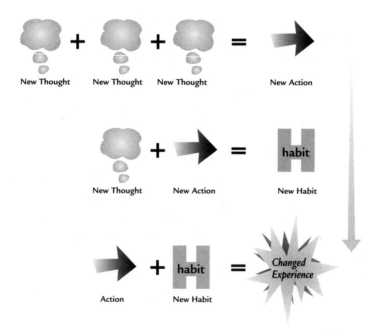

When you were a child, at some point along the way, someone involved in your life started to tell you to brush your teeth. More likely than not, someone showed you how to brush your teeth. Perhaps it was something that you didn't at first understand or do well. Somewhere along the line, the dentist might have reminded you, shown you modified techniques for teeth brushing. And you began to practice. Your caregiver reminded you probably more than once, to brush your teeth. This thought repeated and acted upon, time and time again, brought you to the place where you either acquired the habit of brushing your teeth, or you repeated a different thought and acquired the habit of not brushing your teeth.

> *There is a mechanism which can set us on course to tuning in and living in touch with our true Self. It is a mechanism that you have been using from the time you were born.*

If you're willing, clasp your two hands together and interlace your fingers. Notice which thumb is on top. Notice how that feels. Notice the familiarity of this particular movement. Now, shift all of your fingers up so that the other thumb now rests on top. You might notice it feels peculiar. The reason it feels peculiar is because you have invited a habit to change.

By the same token, if you are in the habit of brushing your teeth, you will notice how peculiar it feels when your teeth are not brushed.

During the course of acquiring our many habits, we may not have been aware that repetition of thought was the method we used to get the habit.

What are the changes you would like in your life? What are the thoughts that you could begin to repeat which would bring you the changes you desire? It is true that the continued and persistent repetition of affirmative thoughts and ideas will bring changes into your experience.

The challenge in this profound and powerful pathway of change is the fact that a new habit never announces itself. You really don't know when you have it. One day, one moment, one millisecond in the course of your life, a new habit, a new change, a new possibility which you set in motion, might arrive in your experience. While we don't know when it will arrive, we do know that out of the Law of the Universe, it will arrive.

In this new approach to life, we are seeking to observe the nature of life and with our intelligence, seek to discern whether or not the human experience in any way mirrors our observations. Through our observations we can see structures which exist in nature and in physical science. For example, we know that if you plant a seed in a prepared soil and nurture it according to certain principles, the seed

We think about the thought and repeat the action and the process goes on until at some point it reaches this invisible place called habit.

must grow. We understand looking at certain physical principles that if you cooperate with their nature, they can be used over and over again without in any way, diminishing the principle.

We all know that water seeks its own level in accord with its own weight. Out of this principle we have discovered the ability to generate hydro-power. Similar laws of physics apply with electricity, for we can use electricity to power any instrument of our choosing so long as we cooperate with the laws of electricity. Understanding the laws of nature, and creating ways to use them, brought us to the technical revolution which we find ourselves in today. The technological changes in the last 20 years probably surpass all of the changes in the 2,000 years of civilized history which have preceded it.

For there are laws of consciousness and belief which can be used impersonally, without in any way diminishing the law, to create changes and advances in the individual experience

The most exciting and new frontier of our time is the frontier of human consciousness. For there are laws of consciousness and belief which can be used impersonally, without in any way diminishing the law, to create changes and advances in the individual experience, your life and mine.

Each of us has a point of view. That point of view is born out of our individuality. Each individual in potential, must indeed be equal. This is what the writers of the Declaration of Independence were inferring when they wrote,

> *We hold these truths to be self-evident, that all men are created equal and they are endowed by their Creator with certain unalienable rights; among these are life, liberty and the pursuit of happiness.*

Yet each individual does not make use of the same potential because the nature of the universal law of consciousness (a fancy term for a simple yet profound reality) is that it can only reflect back to you and me what we give it. Each person is thinking about and functioning

There is no such thing as a neutral thought or state of mind.

from their own beliefs and perceptions. The force and the accuracy with which this mental law receives the direct impress of our thought and acts upon it is determined entirely by the level of faith and conviction in it. Hence you will find throughout the history of the race that the enlightened souls of every tradition have made reference to belief and faith in their lessons for humanity.

Each person believes in something. We have a certain faith when we board an airplane that the airplane will fly. We have a certain faith when we start a car that the internal combustion will remain internal and that by igniting gasoline, we can catch a ride instead of catching on fire. This faith is based upon our understanding that our cooperation with physical laws will produce certain results.

The psychologist believes that their understanding of the nature of mind can be used to bring certain liberating thoughts and ideas to their client. They have faith in the invisible laws of mind or their system of belief about the laws of mind. Out of that faith and conviction they are able to help their clients.

You can observe in your own life those people who believe that life is against them, that there is no underlying intelligence in the Universe, that the only luck they have is bad luck. They continually experience bad luck and claim that life appears to be against them.

Just as the psychologist has faith in their beliefs and get results, people in negation have faith in their beliefs and get results. So the question each of us needs to ask ourselves is what am I believing about life, about myself, about people and about society?

As we've already discussed, the will is a mechanism of choice. Everyone has a will, therefore everyone must make a choice. Your thought, being creative, is acted upon. You are always attracting or repelling something. There is no such thing as a neutral thought or state of mind. The dominant patterns of your thinking become the dominant patterns in your experience. We have a choice. We can anxiously expect the worst, or we can joyously expect the best.

The vast majority of our culture is not awake to the truth of their nature. We are always choosing something. Since so many people are not awake, the choice is being made for us through the attitude of society, the community, and the media. Again, we see the law of mind mimicking laws of nature. We all know that the universe abhors a vacuum and as soon as there is a vacuum, nature seeks to fill it. By the same token, if we don't make a choice, the choice will be made for us.

A little story; the popular psychologist and author, Wayne Dyer, was a guest on a talk show hosted by Sally Jesse Raphael. In his introduction, Wayne claimed that he hadn't had a cold in more than a dozen years. Sally shared this fact as she was introducing him on the show and her first statement to Dr. Dyer was that she didn't believe him. In the solitude and peace of his own belief system, Dr. Dyer pointed out that that was really her problem, not his and that his choice is to express radiant, vibrant and dynamic health. What Dr. Dyer knows is that he does not have to choose to be part of the law of averages or field of statistics which obligates the individual to have colds on a seasonal basis.

In my own experience, on the pathway to acquiring deeper understandings and the amazing power of choice powered by faith, I have overcome, better stated transcended, the statistics about the life expectancy and quality of life for people my age with my history. I have been told by medical professionals that *I was not born to be average and neither were you.* my personal state of health does not reflect itself in the statistics about people with my medical history. I take a certain pride in not fitting into the law of averages. I too choose to live in radiant, vibrant and dynamic health. I was not born to be average and neither were you.

Each of us is born to be an individual. We all have the opportunity to wake up, discover ourselves and make choices from an awakened point of view. No book, no author, no class, or no single experience can give someone a deep and abiding faith in the universe and in themselves. But we can gradually begin to apply certain principles, experience the result of these applications and discern for ourselves a system of belief which will support us on our journey to self realization.

Self-realization is knowing who we are, why we are and living a life in purpose, fulfilled and experiencing a sense of belonging in our own body, in our own skin, on our own planet, in our own time. And all of this coupled with a deep inner conviction that life is good.

Life is good means something more than noticing occasionally it is good, or once in a while it is good, or I once experienced good. It means looking forward every day, in every opportunity, to the ongoing experience of good.

Up to this point, we have been talking about the nature of the universe and how we might use it. As we move further along, we'll talk about practical things that you can do which will, in essence, bring you to the place where you understand the ultimate simplicity that in order to change *Everything works from the inside out.* your experience for the better, you must change your mind. Everything works from the inside out.

These approaches have been called many different things over the last hundred years. But essentially, we are talking about the importance of a new thought. The power which compliments a new thought is faith. The thoughts form the molds into which the substance of faith moves, powered by the conviction within the faith itself, operating upon a natural principle in the universe which through a magnificence of its own, creates our experience. We do not create the magnificence, nor do we create the power, rather we use an already existing creative magnificence. The approach to new thought is affirmation, Spiritual Mind Treatment, meditation and forgiveness.

> *Ye shall know the Truth and the Truth shall set you free.*
>
> Jesus

> *Understanding alone constitutes true salvation.*
>
> E.H.

The key is knowing and understanding.

So get yourself on the path of knowing and understanding, and plan on being there for as long as you can imagine.

CHAPTER SEVEN

REASON AND INTUITION

*Intuition, logic and science don't argue with one another,
in fact, they support one another.*

The starting point of every new action is a thought. Thought acting upon the invisible medium of mind, which is non-local, makes an impress and all depending on the force of the thought, tends to take form in our experience. What gives thought this force? The only answer can be the level of conviction behind the thought. Conviction relates to belief. So how do I give myself a stronger conviction in the direction of my dreams?

As we've already discussed, this atmosphere of conviction is our consciousness. The only effective way of determining the level of our consciousness is by measuring it in our experience, in our actual, practical, day to day life. How much consciousness I have can be determined by the thoughts that I am able to impress upon this invisible law of life which in turn, shows up as demonstrated in my experience.

One of the first definitions of demonstration is to prove by making real. The truth is that every one is demonstrating their beliefs whether they are doing so in awareness or whether they are doing so out of ignorance. Universal laws are not applicable to only some people, they apply to everyone.

The claim then, is that the only authority which can determine whether or not I am, in fact, aligning myself with natural laws and principles, is demonstration. Let us be clear that we are talking about the demonstration of our goals, dreams and desires. For if we are going to use demonstration as an authority, we must be clear of the syllogism in our argument.

Let us not become anxious about the definitions of terms or over complicate the very essence of easy living. This natural law of life goes by many different names. But we are in fact referring to the natural creative process in the Universe.

Artists such as painters know that they must form the intent to paint the picture. They must have paints, canvas, brushes. Yet the painting of the picture is not a mechanical act, it involves a certain creativity. Out of the intent and the groundwork to be able to accomplish the goal, something greater must show up through the artist in order

Conviction relates to belief. So how do I give myself a stronger conviction in the direction of my dreams?

for the painting to become an art work. Ralph Waldo Emerson said that sometimes the muse is too great for the bard. Michaelangelo said that he released the David from the marble.

So the terms of our deductive reasoning always operates on a specific premise, or syllogism.

For example:

Premise 1	*The dog ate the cat*
Assumption	*Dogs eat cats*
Deduction	*All dogs eat cats*

Based on this syllogism, or the information given, we could look at the above deduction and see that there is a certain accuracy. However, you and I recognize that frequently, dogs and cats are in fact very amiable partners. So if we are going to demonstrate our premise that thoughts become things, we must clarify the premise.

Premise 1	*Thoughts become things*
Premise 2	*Thought with conviction becomes things*
Deduction	*It is done unto me as I believe (at the level of my conviction)*

The basic premise of our approach to easy living is we live and move and have our being in a Universal Life. That Universal Life has created us in order so that It can know Itself as us. This means we must consciously recognize ourselves as what It is, in order for the intention to be fulfilled. It is good, therefore It created us to experience good. I must make the decision to orient myself to the reality of Its nature. Orientation is a mental act. And the start of all mental action is thought.

Premise 1	*Life is good*
Premise 2	*I am good*
Deduction	*My life is good*

When I am able to see the simple nature of this syllogism, it becomes necessary for me to adjust all of my thinking and argument toward the *demonstration* of my new premise.

Practically speaking, within my own mentality, I am going to have to move into affirmations and denials, win the argument and get myself to believe the premise. This process of affirming and denying is called realization which leads to living our lives well, being comfortable in our own body and having a deep-seated confidence in the nature of the Universe. This ultimate goal is Self -realization.

We are seeking to bring ourselves to the place that we are alive in the art of feeling, being able to spontaneously feel the aliveness of a true New Thought, a thought so filled with conviction in the perception that it becomes realized. The only process involved between the inner realization of any idea and the actual experience of that thing is nothing more than an anticipated sequence of events.

Think about a time in your life when you were going to visit with an old friend. You began to think about the qualities in that visit, the levels in communication, the ability to laugh, the levels in understanding and the other ineffable qualities associated with a fine friendship. Your sense of belief about the joy in the forthcoming visit is so strong that you are unconcerned with anything in life interrupting your visit.

You go and have the visit, and the experience was even better than your thoughts about it. There was only a logical sequence of events that took place between the thought and the experience.

The things that you didn't think about; the weather, the traffic patterns, busy schedules, the possible complications in visiting somebody in their own home—phones ringing, the TV repair man, or other family routines—all become counter-balanced by your life in vacation mode. None of those things interfered with your intention, because your thought, from the outset, was clear.

We had a thought so filled with conviction in the perception that it became realized.

The reason we can't do this with every thought is because we don't have the feelings and emotions, or the appropriate assigned value, to some of our personal goals, desires and ambitions. This creative law of mind is always receiving what you actually believe, not what you think you believe, or what you would like to believe, but what you actually believe. The philosopher Ernest Holmes said,

> *Man is not what he thinks he is, but he is what he thinks.*

If our lives are not moving in the directions of our dreams, an inquiry into the premise upon which we are operating is not only appropriate, but necessary.

Here's where things get interesting. If you are inquiring into a premise, you are no longer functioning with deductive reasoning, but are in fact functioning with inductive reasoning. Inductive reasoning is an inquiry into the premise. The intelligence of the Universe does not function with inductive reasoning, because the intelligence of the Universe is the premise. The premise does not need to inquire into Itself.

You and I are born in the image of Primary Intelligence and therefore reflect the qualities of this intelligence. While our conscious mind is capable of inducing a question, the nature of our subjective mind, or non-conscious mind, is always responding to our current deductions.

In other words, you cannot ask the nature of life to stop responding to you and mirroring back the sum total of your beliefs simply because you are involved in an inquiry and have not arrived at a clear conclusion. On some level, it is a pleasant thought to imagine that we could put life on hold while we seek to discover whether or not we believe in it. But Universal Life has no choice but to exist with or without your belief in It. As you are created in Its image, Life always responds to life. The creative mechanism of Life must always respond to you. It responds to you at the level of your current deductions.

Ultimately, we seek to get ourselves to the place where, at the deepest level of our argument, we believe through our experiences that life is good, that the Universe is for us and our place in eternity is guaranteed. Yet, if we have not arrived at a deep level of conviction or embodiment of these concepts, we continue to doubt, even though we may not have arrived at a final conclusion.

The mechanism of life, which responds to your current subjective conclusions, has no choice but to reflect back to you in your experience, a God that may be good or a God that may be random or somehow out of touch with Its creation. This might look like, sometimes I'm lucky and sometimes I'm unlucky.

There is a place at the center of our existence which is the source of the direct revelation of Truth from the essence of the very life within us. In the human being, revelation from this source moves through us as intuition. Sometimes we know and we just know that we know. Pure intuition is always accurate and does not err. You and I sometimes find it difficult to distinguish between intuition and a hunch. In the early stages of our quest to live in close contact with our intuition, it is probably a good idea to begin with listening to your hunches. A hunch is our getting the glimpse of a much stronger force

Intuition, logic and science do not argue with one another, they support each other.

which is pure intuition. The only way to cultivate a strengthened ability to perceive our clear intuition is by bringing our intellect into harmony with the pure Intelligence of intuition.

> *...there is hardly any doubt that intuition is the real source of knowledge, different from the role of senses and reason. It is especially indispensable in the apprehension of those aspects of the true reality which are inaccessible to the sense and to reason.*
>
> Pitirim Sorokin

The source of intuition is pure Intelligence. The source of your logical intelligent mind is also pure Intelligence. Intuition, logic and science do not argue with one another, they support each other.

The way to harmonize intellect and intuition is to inquire into our doubts. As you look further and deeper into your doubts and intelligently meet the argument or assuage the fear, the doubt will dissipate. In fact, it shall be transformed through the intelligence which is in you.

Perhaps as you approach the last few pages of this chapter, as we have been discussing reason and intuition, you have become discouraged and don't feel that you understand all of this, or that you will ever understand all of this. This is self-doubt.

What is it that you don't think you understand? Looking deeper still, why do I have to understand all of this about reasoning when my quest is to feel the presence of life and to make my life easier? A possible answer is, I don't.

What I have to discover is that life responds to my beliefs. Do I believe that life is intelligent? Do I believe there are structures in the Universe that operate intelligently? Do I believe that I am inter-related with the cause of life, the Spirit of life? Am I related to the intelligent structures of life? Perhaps I am willing to see that the physical structures of every material thing are based on the organization of energy. I am a physical structure, I have energy, I, therefore, must be related to all of life. I am committing myself to a deeper realization of my relationship with the whole. All of this has revealed itself through my inquiry into my life.

Becoming comfortable is about thinking and feeling. Somewhere in the course of your inquiry, that which you think and that which you feel shall merge. At the point of that convergence we will be in the active demonstration of our new belief, based on the new syllogism, the new premise which we have presented. The creative mechanism of life within each one of us automatically responds to our new deduction, or the conclusion of the new premise.

When we establish a premise which works toward the fulfillment of our goals, dreams and desires, the creative mechanism of life begins to make our life easier.

When Einstein was asked what the most important question was, he replied, "Is the Universe friendly?"

If the Universe is friendly then God is on my side. As there is only one Verse (Uni-verse) then I am what God is.

God is…	I am what God is
God is good…	God is Life
I am life…	My life is good
Hey, this is cool…	Cool just IS

CHAPTER EIGHT

TOO GOOD TO BE TRUE

I am radiant, vibrant, dynamic health.

Since you are reading this book, its a fair assumption that you already have lots of habits. If you've gotten this far, its a fair assumption that you are one of a special group of people who is motivated to learn and to grow and to discover themselves.

One of the most profound and powerful tools in the pathway of our transformation is the technique of affirmation. Affirmations can be used to begin to change negative habit patterns. However, if we choose to use an affirmation (in the area of health for example) such as, "I am radiant, vibrant, dynamic health" effectively, we must also begin to pay attention to our thought processes and our reactions to this affirmation. Instead of following the fear, we make a choice and we choose to remind ourselves "I am radiant, vibrant, dynamic health."

We obviously must do this more than once. We must do it every time we find ourselves participating in fear about our health. The constant repetition will begin to set a new habit into motion and we will notice those passing pains are fewer and that we begin to take them for what they are, as signals to our awareness.

All pain is a message. The reason we have pain, is to get a message from our body to our awareness. The flow of information from body to awareness is a two-way street. Information also flows from our awareness into our body. So we discover that an affirmation is not simply a nice little warm, namby-pamby, happy thought, it is literally a starting point for the restructuring of certain aspects of our physiology.

My friend, Michael Beckwith, tells the story of a man who grew up with a lack of self-esteem. He could not find anything in his life that spoke of happiness and joy. He thought about his parental upbringing, he thought about his schooling and his inner monologue went something like this, "…life was bad and it treated me very harshly in my youth."

So one day, he decided to try this affirmation: he said, *I have always had a happy childhood.* He began to remember moments in his life that he had totally forgotten. He remembered that his grandmother loved him and use to make a special apple pie whenever he came to visit. He remembered that his father, even in teasing him about his size and his big ears, was doing it in jest. He remembered a best friend that he had all through elementary school and high school. He started

> *You are one of a special group of people who is motivated to learn and to grow and to discover themselves.*

to recall all these magnificent and wonderful moments in his life that were glossed over and obscured by this predominant thought pattern that life was bad and that he never had a happy childhood. By saying the affirmation, *I have always had a happy childhood,* suddenly what burst into his awareness were all these moments that were there but were hidden away. He didn't have to change his childhood, he didn't have to change anything. He just had to look at it from a different vantage point. Suddenly he accessed a tremendous esteem, a tremendous self-love, and became empowered. It all began with him saying, *I have always had a happy childhood.*

We would do well to get in the habit of repeating affirmations.

"I am radiant, vibrant, dynamic health."

"More and more money is flowing into my life and I deserve it."

"I love life and life loves me!"

"I am clear in my decision. I know what I want and I act upon it."

Put one on your refrigerator. Put one on your mirror. Put one in your car. Learn them! Repeat them! Use them!

As you can see, what resulted from the use of the affirmation, *I've always had a happy childhood,* was a deeper remembering of the actual experience rather than a surface perception of the experience.

We are dealing in a Mind that always responds to our thought. We are always actively attracting or repelling something. The question becomes, are we pleased with what we may be attracting? Do we have regrets about what we might be pushing away? Using affirmation effectively, requires a willingness to listen to our own thinking.

For example, for the person who constantly goes around saying *I can never remember names*, it will be impossible to get better at remembering names. To use an affirmation effectively, we would have to change the dialogue and move 180 degrees in the opposite direction of the negation. Perhaps, *I'm getting better at remembering names all the time, but right now I can't recall so and so's name,* would be an appropriate affirmation. This kind of technique gives us permission to honestly admit a circumstance without affirming its need to continually reoccur.

At the point of our self awareness, we discovered that we are able to think and that each of us selects our own thoughts. We have moved into the creative process. You and I do not create things, we use a Creativity. As long as we are automatically and inescapably using the Creative capacity, we may as well use it productively and creatively.

Affirmations do not necessarily set our course. They are very effective tools in helping to adjust the course so that we remain more "centered" in pursuing the direction of our goals, dreams and desires. Affirmations steer us toward Self-reliance and help us avoid beliefs which create circumstances that are taking us off course. If you have decided it is your right to be healthy, make it a habit to remind yourself—*I am radiant, vibrant, dynamic health.* Even if you are not clear, repeating this won't hurt, and it may even help on the path to a richer life.

CHAPTER NINE

MONEY

*We pay for everything with either spiritual
or mental coin.*

Ernest Holmes

Money is certainly one of the most deeply charged subjects in our lives. Those who have it want more of it. Those who don't have it dream of it. Life without it is virtually impossible.

One of the greatest misunderstandings in our culture is that it is possible to think and grow rich. If you are familiar with the book by Napoleon Hill, you recognize that although there is a great deal of wisdom in the book, there is much more involved in the process of becoming rich than simply dreaming or hoping, or even thinking. As we have discussed in many places throughout this book, we recognize that thoughts, without a supporting belief system, are insufficient to change any circumstance or situation. Thoughts accompanied with **conviction** are indeed a powerful transformative force.

*My words fly up but my thoughts remain below,
words without thoughts will not to heaven go.*

Shakespeare

Perhaps it is human nature to look for the easy solution to every circumstance. Yet, the idea that there is, "something for nothing," would presume a Universe that is disorganized and random. Fortunately for us, we live in an intelligent, structured Universe. So the challenge is to organize our own belief systems to match the given structure of the Universe. Here's some important news: the Universe will never go broke!

So let's take a look. The various astronauts on the Apollo mission looked out upon the void of space and saw the magnificent green-blue ball hanging in the emptiness and recognized that this ball is the living

One of the greatest misunderstandings in our culture is that it is possible to think and grow rich.

organism known as the planet Earth. It's hard to imagine, looking at the one planet, the millions of individual lives, the variety of life forms and the billions of challenges which face life on the planet. Yet, the planet lives, the solar system remains intact and, as you are currently reading this book, new planets, new solar systems and new galaxies are right now being formed. All of this to remind us that with or without your consenting opinion, existence will continue to exist because it is self-sustaining, self-governing and self-supplying. There is more than enough supply. There is more than enough money.

The philosopher Buckminster Fuller suggests that there is more than enough food to feed everyone on the planet and there is more than enough water. New technologies are revealing to us potential alternative energy sources which could never be diminished. The challenge is to find ourselves immersed in the feedback loop of unlimited supply. The first step in this direction is to recognize and understand the law of compensation.

Emerson said that on the subject of compensation, life is way ahead of religion. It could accurately be said that life is also ahead of science and philosophy. For every act there is a reaction and for every act of giving, there is a compensation. It is a great challenge to the human mind to rely on this law of compensation. The law of compensation is the same law that receives the impress of our thought and acts upon it. It works in the area of compensation as though it were its own law; for every act of giving there is a compensation. If we are seeking a greater compensation, we need to establish a clearer vision of our right level of giving. In order to live the life of our dreams, we are going to have to do our part. Getting a clearer vision of our right level of giving and establishing within our own minds our right to be compensated is a purpose in our quest.

We need to bear in mind that regardless of our position in the world of finances, there is no place of ultimate arrival. I remember in the '70s, driving down Sunset Boulevard with the windows down and the sun-roof open, singing my heart out to the rock and roll that was blasting on the radio. On my left, as I was adjacent to the Beverly Hills Hotel, there was a large, highly polished Rolls Royce Cornice. The lady driving the car was adorned with diamonds which were quite visible from the next lane. She rolled down her passenger window, wiped the tears from her eyes and asked me if I was really as happy as I appeared. My answer was *"Yes!"*

Here's some important news: the Universe will never go broke!

Money cannot buy happiness. Money cannot buy awareness. Money cannot buy the only salvation that our soul will ever know, which is understanding. Having said this, let's put our attention on how we might get more money.

As we have discussed earlier, life is always responding to our current level of understanding based on the deductions which we present to life. Are you presenting a limited premise about money to the law of your own existence? Perhaps you believe that work is hard and you have to work hard in order to make money. Perhaps you believe there is only one way for you to make money. Perhaps you believe other people have all the luck. Perhaps you believe being rich makes you arrogant. Perhaps you believe good fortune never comes your way. Perhaps you believe the above list is an absolute fallacy and the truth is that I love what I do and love is fulfilling my goals. Perhaps you believe that no matter what you do, you make money. Perhaps you believe that every dollar you spend is a giving to the law of circulation and therefore is coming back to you multiplied.

One of the craziest ideas of all time is that money is the root of all evil.

At this point, you should be able to discern which of the above mentioned thoughts are valuable and which ones are worthless. If you are functioning with worthless thoughts, they will show up in your experience as being worth even less.

We've got a lot of crazy ideas. What do we have to do with these crazy ideas? We have to change our minds. One of the craziest ideas of all time is that money is the root of all evil. Let's get honest, **NO MONEY** is the root of all evil.

If you were exposed to the idea that money is bad, most likely that came from the bible and the bible does not say anywhere that money is the root of evil. In Timothy it says *The **love** of money is the root of all evil.* This means money is not for its own sake, but is a tool to help us achieve our goal which is to express a rich, comfortable, easy life, which fulfills our purpose. Looking at your own life,

Change is inevitable. Growth is optional.

would you rather be in a miserable environment, or a positive environment? Would you rather be in an opulent environment, or a poor environment? Would you rather transport yourself safely or dangerously?

If you want prosperity on the outside, you've got to change on the inside. Some may say that would be a lot of work. I don't believe there are any tricks. I don't believe bending spoons or walking over coals, or surviving any deep emotional catharsis will make you richer. Changing your mind so you can change your experience means that YOU have to change your mind and YOU have to do the work.

Change is inevitable. Growth is optional. We need to start choosing to grow, which means we have to start recognizing the divinity of money. Money is substance which is used for exchange which is used for flow. When money is used constructively, it is good and it is very good. We need to bring to awareness to the concept that every time we spend a dollar in this society, we are investing into this economy. We need to understand that our investments into a good idea are paying a dividend.

What is the foundation on which our economy is built? The foundation of this country is essentially life, liberty and the pursuit of happiness. If you went to a financial advisor and he told you he had some ideas to invest in, one was doom and despair, lack, limitation and fear and one was life, liberty and the pursuit of happiness, which do you think would be the better investment?

Life, liberty and the pursuit of happiness and money invested or money spent toward that purpose is a sound investment.

The soul is not a compensation, but a life.
Ralph Waldo Emerson

We need to start readjusting our thinking about the bills we pay, about the cost of our survival, and begin to realize that we are investing into our lives and that each one of us is worth the investment. You are deserving of the good things that happen in your life and you are worthy of the compensation which you receive. When you are willing to think constructively, it will serve you by raising your self-esteem which will raise your sense of value. This greater sense of self-worth will result in a greater compensation.

If you are going to drink a glass of water, and you have a choice between water that is murky and cloudy and water which is clear, which one will you drink? Is that a complicated decision for you, or did it come easily, spontaneously and naturally? Water to the living organism is necessary, and the living organism has an innate ability to choose the cup with more value.

You and I offer a murky picture to life, and we wonder why life chooses the other person who was offering the clear picture. It is the natural order of the Universe for innate intelligence to select the highest and clearest alternative, always. Intelligence always flows to the highest level of thought which is offered. You and I create thoughts which form molds which the Universe fills. The more specific the mold, the more specific will be the casting which comes from the mold.

What do you mean you want more money? The scientist turned mystic, Guy Merchie, said, "All flowers and blossoms apparently without exception, are reproductive organs." Look at the reproductive organs of flowers. Every aspect of nature conspires that one flower may produce thousands of more flowers behind it. The orange and the

You have to remember life is going to change.

watermelon are laden with seeds that will bear more trees and plants that will produce more fruit. Look how the Universe is always giving back to Itself, because the Universe represented in nature, is for Itself. It's in charge. It chooses through pre-established laws in nature to bless and multiply Itself. In the Old Testament it doesn't talk about some blessings, it talks about showers of blessings.

In as much as the life force dwells within you, you are an intricate part of nature and within you there is an innate desire to reproduce, to multiply and to establish and re-establish good and more good for you and for all those who may follow. The creative process within you demands that you offer a starting point for creativity. The starting point is your own consciousness.

It doesn't do me any good to know that I am a place in consciousness, because I have my life, and my life has pain, and my life has doubts, and my life has fears and my life has the greatest problem of all, !!!**@@!**! **BILLS**.

The good news is consciousness may be expanded. We understand consciousness, which is unseen, becomes experience. Consciousness is built by thought. The desire to transcend pains, doubts, fears and to be freed from the burden of unmanageable finances is good. These desires reflect a willingness within you to change.

It must be your decision to use this urge creatively as a starting point for growth. It is up to you to decide to be creative or to create stress. Jack Canfield, the self-esteem author and lecturer, offers this simple formula:

$$E + R = O$$

Event + Response = Outcome

You have to remember life is going to change. Change is inevitable, growth is optional. We need to start choosing to grow. We need to realize that our money issues are in our experience as an opportunity to grow. In the big picture, life is about a lot more than money issues.

As we've talked about before, life is an inside job. It's built from the invisible which we call consciousness and comes into form as our experience. How's your money consciousness? What are your goals, dreams and desires? What do you mean you want more money? It has become evident that the Universe is not withholding from you. The opportunity exists in this moment to align yourself with the natural tendency in the Universe to multiply.

The opportunity exists in this moment to align yourself with the natural tendency in the Universe to multiply.

Let's take a look at how we might begin to clarify our desires. Let's talk about Bud Wiser. Bud sat down and wrote 5 things he wanted to do with money.

1. I want to be debt free
2. I want a house
3. I want to increase my cash flow
4. I want a new car
5. I want a new computer

Bud, are you going to buy the house all cash? Are you going to buy the car all cash? Why do you want a new computer?

Bud wanted a new computer in order to be able to improve his output as a graphic designer which is the way he produces his cash flow. He wants a new car so that he can comfortably move from one client to the next. He can lease a car and deduct a significant portion of his lease toward his business. He doesn't want to pay all cash for a house, he wants a conventional mortgage. Bud's number one goal was to be debt free. Every other goal was in conflict with his first goal.

There is a law that receives the direct impress of your thought and acts upon it by returning to the giver a corresponding experience. What the heck is an intelligent law going to do with this list? Whose job is it to clarify their understanding? Is God confused? Could Bud stand to be a little bit wiser?

What Bud, you and I need to do is clarify our focus and establish a direction in our lives which the fulfillment of our goals will compliment.

Only as you know that you have a right to live your life and fulfill your purpose, that through focusing on your desire to fulfill that purpose and then establishing goals, dreams and desires that complement your focus shall you experience easy living, surrounded by an abundance that reflects your personal view of success.

So let's see if we can help Bud and if Bud can help us to clarify the picture.

In order to clarify his goals Bud hired Paul Rather, who is a professional intent-clarifier. Paul had a brief interview with Bud:

Paul Rather

Do you like the graphic design business?

Bud Wiser

Oh, yah. It's very creative, and I love to see my client's faces when they are inspired by a particular presentation.

Rather

So you would say that you like to be creative, and you like to be helpful.

Wiser

Ya'.

Rather

Would you say that this is your life's purpose?

Wiser

Well no, I'm not even sure I have a life's purpose.

Rather

Well would you say that your business has a purpose?

Wiser

Ya'. To meet the client's need and get paid for doing the job well.

Rather

What happened to the joy in seeing your client's face light up? Isn't that one of your favorite things?

Wiser

Well, yeah, I guess it is, I never thought of it that way.

Rather

So what would be a better statement of purpose for your business?

Wiser

Well, I seek to lay out ideas in such a way that it inspires clients to new levels of success.

Rather

So, you're in the inspiration business?

Wiser

(smiling)
I guess so.

Rather

What's important in your life?

Wiser

Being creative, inspiring, and helping others to succeed and getting paid.

Rather

Do me a favor, Bud, rewrite your list of goals within the focus of your purpose.

My purpose is to be creative, inspiring and help others to succeed.

1. I want a new computer
2. I want to increase my cash flow.
3. I want a new car
4. I want a house
5. I want to comfortably manage my assets and debts

The first three goals are directly related to the business. Ultimately, all of the goals compliment each other toward the fulfillment of Bud's life purpose.

It is insufficient to say, "I want more money." It's our charge to figure out who we would Rather be.

The way to discover your life purpose begins with believing that you have one. We live in an ordered Universe, you are part of that order. You have a place in the Universe and you have a right to discover it.

It is important that we begin a quest of self discovery. What do I want out of life? What do I want out of my work? What is my version of a life well-lived? What is the primary focus of my life?

If you can't be sure of the overall focus of your life, then where is the focus now? Get that focus clear, remembering that you always have the right to change your mind. Our unclear mental concept is reflecting back in our lives as an unclear, sometimes good and some-

The way to discover your life purpose begins with believing that you have one.

times bad kind of life. We have a right to express a life of ever-expanding awareness and ever-expanding good.

Oftentimes we are afraid to establish a focus, because we fear at some level we might be wrong, or through our focus we might leave out some vital aspect of ourselves. Imagine yourself looking through a camera lens. In the center of the lens is a little box, which is where you aim the camera in order to focus. Yet the picture includes much more than simply the focal point. The entire picture exists because we chose a focal point. Without that focal point the camera doesn't know what kind of picture to make. If you shoot the picture without focusing, there's a very good possibility its going to be fuzzy.

I'd rather be wiser.

CHAPTER TEN

CHANGE

Change is inevitable, growth is optional.

Time, in and of itself, is not real. Yet, whether or not we go into profound scientific explanations about the non-existence of time, you and I are faced daily with the prospect of getting things accomplished within a certain period of time. Yet it would be impossible to imagine the Creative Intelligence of the Universe being in a hurry.

Has there ever been a galaxy that has not been created on time? Do we know of suns burning out too soon or lasting too long? Did God misguide the orbit of certain planets? It would appear that from the natural order of things, everything is on time. Yet in the world of daily life, we have created deadlines, time frames and schedules which cause us to put a great deal of stress on our lives. We're running out of time...

From the point of view of creation, the only possible moment to create or to act is now. It has been said that perhaps time exists simply to prevent everything from happening at once. Scientifically, time is often referred to as that space it takes for objects to move from one place to another. Since the Universe Itself is in all space, and it seems to exist even where space is not, then the Universe, or God, or Spirit, or Ralph, does not seem to be caught up in time.

If the Universe is not pressured by time, and we exist out of the intelligence of the Universe, there must be a way that we can move in time with the same ease and comfort and grace as pure thought. Thought is not encumbered by space or sequence, so it seems the natural key to unlocking the pressure of time has something to do with thought.

If I can resolve the pressures and conflicts in my world back to thought, and then get my thinking clear, free and unpressured, I will begin to experience a kind of "slick 50," or reduced-friction way of living.

Isn't it true that we are always looking for some kind of magic formula that would somehow smooth everything out, something that would reduce the wear and tear and simply cause us to be able to move around more gracefully within the pressures of everyday living? Yet, when it comes time to free our thinking, we have developed a myriad of ways by which we can do virtually everything, except establish a **new** thought.

As you are reading this book I recognize that you are an evolving soul and have engaged the power of your mind for the purpose of making your life better. Yet how many habits of avoidance do you actively practice? How many hours of television do you watch a day? What kind of substances do you take which alter your state of consciousness? How often do you meditate, or better stated, how often do you avoid meditating?

It would be impossible to imagine the Creative Intelligence of the Universe being in a hurry.

It seems to be a fairly natural human response to resist change. Yet the absolute and unavoidable reality on this plane of existence is that change is inevitable.

Part of our struggle with time is our resistance to change. Spirit is absolute and, in Its own nature, must be perfect. It created me. It is all things, I must be what It is. There is nothing else that I could possibly be. So in my own nature, I must also be perfect. Yet all of us know that perfection is not the goal. All of us know that what we are really trying to do is to be the most human being that we can be. Because if we would seek to be the most human being that we can be, we will discover that a true pathway to spirituality is to reveal our humanity. The human gives way to the Divine. To be human and to be spiritual are the same.

No one is asking you to be perfect. Yet it is essential to personal fulfillment that you discover the motivation within you to be the most **YOU** that you can be. The Divine idea of you is greater than the concepts you hold for yourself.

Ernest Holmes said, "We are the result of a personal experience, plus the collective experience, plus the impact of the Universal Mind, on the consciousness of everything." Did you know you were that much? We are part personal experience and that means all of our personal lives, all our psychological stuff, everything that has ever happened to us as individuals. We are also part of the collective experience. We are human beings and we are in the human experience and the human experience is acting upon us. In addition to all of this, we are being pushed, driven or evolved forward. So we are working with the personal experience, the collective experience and the experience of the race, as well as the intention of evolution. Evolution is moving forward.

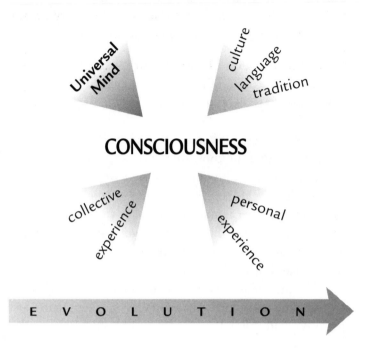

You and I, if we want to set ourselves free from the limited experience of the race, must begin to make certain decisions. We must begin to clear our way back to the Source of our existence. We are going to have to step through the stuff, and go

The only possible moment to create or to act is now.

back to the Source where It is whole, complete and perfect and undisturbed by the inaccurate misconceptions of the race. This stepping is a mental act.

We can begin to create a new reality. We can demonstrate a new vigor, a new health. We can move beyond prognosis and diagnosis. We can move beyond fear, because in Spirit the only thing that happens is the fresh moment of creation.

We are going to have to accept the inevitable reality of change. We are afraid of change because we are afraid of breaking the symmetry and moving into the unknown. We pose an interesting enigma to life when we want things to be different, and we don't want anything to change. Even the supreme Intelligence has trouble with this little paradox.

We have this cute little idea that everything should always be in a perfect linear order, always revealing itself rationally, in a one-two-three, ABC kind of manner. When something goes instantly from A to N, we don't know what to do, and everything seems strange.

We pose an interesting enigma to life when we want things to be different, and we don't want anything to change.

One of the most profound symbols for the wholeness of life is a circle, without beginning and without end, all inclusive and able to expand. For the moment, allow yourself to be symbolized as a circle. If you seek to grow, I suggest that as human beings, we do not grow symmetrically or uniformly. The process of your personal growth is liable to cause you to change forms. You are probably going to experience distortion in the process of your development. By distort, I mean things, circumstances and situations are going to change.

Do you remember in the 60's and 70's, they had those lava lamps? Do you remember those little bubble things and how the bubble would stretch to look like an 8, and then another shape, and then it would begin to rise as a sphere.

Our growth is like that. In order for us to grow, we must break the symmetry.

No matter how organized, or neatly ordered we have our little world, if we want to grow, we are going to have to allow it to change form.

Have you ever moved from one place to another? Perhaps as you were organizing the move, you knew it would be tough. You knew it would be disorienting, yet your desire to move was motivated by the possibility of things being better. You faced the challenge. You went through the process and, eventually, things did get better.

Well, life is like that. You have to let go of the old place and go through a process to get to a better place. My desk is a lot like life. Maybe your desk is too. I have a sense of order, I like for things to be orderly. I start things out on a Monday and everything is in its right place. By the time Monday afternoon rolls around, I can't find a pencil, even though there is one on my desk, someplace. But I have learned to be confident that I have the ability to restore the symmetry. Out of all of that movement of paper and notes and memos, there has

The most disorienting, time consuming, stress creating, unproductive way of living is to seek to hold everything in its place.

been an expansion. In a peculiar kind of way, there is an order in breaking the symmetry. The most disorienting, time consuming, stress creating, unproductive way of living is to seek to hold everything in its place. Change is the way the Universe expands.

If I am going to become comfortable in time it is necessary that I adjust myself to the reality of change. This kind of thinking may be different than what you are familiar with; and it is true that old habit patterns of thought do not die easily. But you can change your mind, and you can change your experience, because you can think.

> *I will think, I will will and I will act. But guide my thinking, willing and action so I may do what You would have me do.*
>
> Yogananda

If we will invite the Universe into every decision, into every action, into every reaction, if we will look with our conscious awareness to feel the presence, to see Its wisdom, we will begin to see a natural order born out of change. Change will no longer be something we fear, it will be something we invite.

Isn't it interesting that the Universe acts like its breathing. Expanding out into awareness, regressing into a different order. Every time we grasp a new idea, every time we touch a new possibility, that far we can go.

There is no such thing as a problem without a solution. There is no such thing as not enough time when you have the courage to remember this:

I always have time to do the important things.

CHAPTER ELEVEN

COMPENSATION

On the subject of compensation, life is
ahead of theology.

Emerson

Ignorance is not bliss and there is no such thing as something for nothing. Ignorance contributes to all of your problems because you cannot use principles which you don't know about. The advancement of our awareness is dependent upon our discovery of deeper, unseen, transcendent forces. That's why when you truly know better, you will do better. When you really know there is a law of life which responds to your every thought you will start to think about what you think about.

Let's be reminded we are talking about something more than thoughts being things. We are talking about thought as the *cause* of things. Thought, working through attitude, becomes your experience. Many of us have spent 30, 40 or more years establishing attitudes which don't serve us and work against the direction of our dreams, goals and desires.

We come upon a very simple, yet profound idea: our thinking is active, and there is no such thing as a thought that is not acted upon. So, what if we have a new idea—we want to be uplifted, we want to feel the presence of a Life Force that is with us and for us? Yet, curiously, we only want to put our attention on It, maybe once or twice a week, and we wonder how come we don't experience It all the time?

Fortunately, we don't have to spend as long in changing our minds as we did in creating the original patterns because in the change, we are functioning with a new level of awareness. In our change we have a deeper level of knowledge that there is a force acting upon our thought which has been there all along. We just weren't aware of it.

There's a funny thing about awareness, you discover you have it, then you discover you had it all along, you just weren't aware of it.

Why is it that we always look for and are attracted to the free thing? At a deeper level of inquiry, we recognize that a two-for-one sale is not really two for one because the price of the first item is usually elevated. The free meal isn't free, because it requires the purchase of another meal. There are countless examples of people who have won the lottery, who within a few short years, have nothing left. Why is it

> *Our thinking is active and there is no such thing as a thought that is not acted upon.*

that our school systems teach a concept of the Universe which we know is outdated and inaccurate? Dr. Melvin Morse, in his recent book *Transformed by the Light* says, "Our schools still teach the concept of a billiard ball universe that is made out of atoms, when we know it is made out of light." Why do I ask these questions? Because they illustrate how we are afraid to grow and move into a new awareness.

We know things about the Universe we didn't know before. We know that the pre-quantum view of a Universe filled with billiard balls smashing around each other making matter, isn't the way it is. Energy and matter are equal and interchangeable. Everything is, in essence, light and we are slow to change our textbooks to give our children a new awareness.

One of the most profound discoveries of this century has yet to be integrated into our awareness because the implications require a radical shift in the understanding of consciousness. There is a vast amount of scientific evidence to verify the reality that the observer in any given experiment affects the outcome. This means the consciousness looking at anything has an impact on the thing or object of its perception.

Each one of us is a participant and observer of our own lives. What we expect as we are observing the things we are participating in has a profound effect on our experience. The implication is that attitude is much more important than we may have realized. This led the philosopher, clergymen, physician, and music scholar, Albert Schweitzer to say,

> *The greatest discovery of any generation is that human beings can alter their lives by altering their attitudes of mind.*

To change an old habit pattern of thought that actually believes it is possible to get something for nothing might be a difficult and challenging endeavor. Yet, it is necessary because we live in a Universe that moves from cause to effect, from giving to receiving, from the inside to the outside. Our incessant demand to change things on the outside, without changing on the inside, will never be answered, because it disagrees with the natural order of the Infinite Intelligence whose primary law is harmony and order.

When we continue to struggle from the outside to the outside, we will never touch the wellspring of solution. The problem might change, names and the circumstances may be different, but the same problem will occur again and again. Many of us have experienced this reality in our personal lives as we have dumped one relationship for the next to get the same person and issues with a different name.

We all have natural gifts. To access these gifts, we need to apply a definite knowledge of technique where necessary. The natural gifts are reason, will and action. Through the application of reason, and applied technique in the use of will, we can be led to action which is guided by the highest faculty within the human being, intuition.

The philosopher Ernest Holmes speaks of the possibility of intuition being for humans what instinct is for the animal.

> *The Lord: It is suchness but suchness neither grows nor diminishes. (He) who repeatedly and often dwells in mental activities connected with that Suchness comes near to the supreme enlightenment.*
> The Wisdom of Buddhism

The pathway to intuition is through participating with the qualities of being. Being can only be defined by the qualities in life which are eternally present: peace, love, beauty, humility, joy and humor, to name but a few.

As we begin to access these qualities, a deeper sense of self is revealed. We have chosen to use the highest power within us which we access by choosing to live from love and all of the qualities in life that are life-giving and constructive. In this way, we will naturally participate with the flow of life, and the flow acts as though it goes in front of us and makes the way clear.

Not long ago, I was in my health club getting ready to exercise. I walked into the locker room to find myself surrounded by two young urban professionals on the pathway to duking it out. Each was arguing with the other about how bad their day had been, and about how mad they were over why and how the towel was on the floor. I found myself in the middle of this field of energy which definitely felt chaotic and my instinct was to do something. My intuition said to me, "Do you want to get punched?" I made an inner choice to dwell on suchness.

Transformation happens out of simply knowing the Truth.

Suchness knows of harmony, it knows right and good, it knows the towel on the floor is insufficient cause for violence, it knows how to restore itself in poise, in balance, in joy, in life-givingness at all times. This is where my attention went as my mouth remained shut. Within a matter of a few seconds, the energy shifted. Within a matter of minutes, the one man extended his hand to the other man, identified himself, apologized, they shook hands and the situation was resolved.

I did not do it. I simply offered an avenue through which the intelligence of the Universe was given room to move.

I can't give my best unless I have room to move.
                                        John Mayall, musician.

Transformation happens out of simply knowing the Truth. You are an instrument through which conscious intelligence may move.

The gifts are reason, will and action. When you are willing to be an instrument for Innate Intelligence, the Universe will graciously use you to play Its music.

Oftentimes we are asking the Universe to show us the way, to show us a sign, when, in truth, we should be asking, "Show me how to read the signs!" Because the signs are everywhere present. It is impossible for life to respond to your demand for something-for-nothing when all things in life are a compensation, a reflection of what you have already given.

The entire intent of this book is to suggest that we should re-orient our system of thinking to become inspiration-based instead of desperation-based. In order to expand our experience, we need to expand our awareness. This is the pathway to easy living.

In some of the Eastern traditions, you pay your doctor when you and your family are well. You actually pay the doctor every month or two, because you and your family are doing well. The doctors in these cultures are there to support you in your doing well. When we are doing well we pay, when we are not doing well, we do not pay. It seems in our culture, that we have our

The consciousness that got you where you are will not get you where you want to go.

wellness system a little mixed up. We seek to handle everything from the place of desperation, until such time as we are in crisis and then, and only then, do we turn to an authority greater than our isolated, separated, ego-self.

A good example of this was after the recent California earthquake, when the attendance level at various religious spiritual centers (by whatever name), increased. It would appear that the overwhelming power revealed by what feels like the entire Earth moving, reminded the residents of a Power much greater than their own. So out of desperation, people sought to connect with a deeper level of inspiration.

The consciousness that got you where you are will not get you where you want to go. This means we must move away from judgment and competition, self-centered egocentricity and into unconditional love and synchronicity.

We are going to have to make a commitment to have fun, to be joyful, to truly live our lives and to support the Universe in ourselves, in each other, and in the Planet, all of which vibrate with the same life force.

The level of tension that *you* present to life is going to come back to *you* in every situation, regardless of the label *you* give it.

When we are desperately lonely, we become willing to pay for a relationship seminar. When we have too much money, we are willing to pay for money management. When our psychological problems are desperately apparent, we are willing to pay for a therapist. When our spiritual needs are not being fulfilled, we reluctantly pay for our spiritual support.

We would be far better off to start with the idea of wellness, to commit our lives to inspiration and to be willing to strengthen our health, our well being and our prosperity in consciousness before there is a crisis in experience.

This means that we are going to have to release the idea that you can get something for nothing and you're going to have to pay first. An unusual concept, but if we pay in advance with thoughts and attitudes, the dividends will be rich and the investment is guaranteed blue chip.

CHAPTER TWELVE

RELATIONSHIP

If you want a friend, be a friend.
Ralph Walso Emerson

At first glance, the subject of relationships seems complex, emotional, charged and able to reach every extreme between absolute bliss and absolute terror.

This book is about easy living. So the appropriate question is how can I make my relationships easy? If I am longing for relationship, how do I find myself in positive and loving relationships?

You may be familiar with what is now being called the holographic theory. This theory is based on the fact that you can take a photographic plate which has captured a three-dimensional image and smash it into any number of pieces; then present any fragment of the plate to the laser light and the entire three-dimensional image will be visible.

While the term holography might be a new term, and the concept of holographic images a new technology, what this theory suggests is certainly not new. The brilliant American thinker, Ralph Waldo Emerson spoke of the Whole being in the part, and the part being in the Whole. Philosophers have referred to the microcosm and the macrocosm. All relationships are actually a reflection of your relationship to the Whole. And the sum total of your current relationships reflects your relationship with the Whole.

*Is it possible our entire lives are a manifestation of
what we think about God?*

Anonymous

The point is, we need to discover what ideas about relationship we have to the Whole that are being reflected in our
relationships to the parts.

The focus in our lives must begin with courting and devel-
oping a relationship with the qualities of Life. It makes no
difference whether you are spiritual-based or whether you
are relationship-based. In other words, if you are seeking a
place to share your kindness, or a place to be nurtured, or a
place to have fun, or a place to appreciate beauty, or a place
to enjoy sensuality, those qualities need to be nurtured in
the total of your relationship with Life, with other people,
with other groups, and most importantly, with yourself.
Experiences in the physical world mirror back to us an opportunity to adjust our focus.

Some of us want relationship to begin, some of us want relationship to be improved, some of us want more relationships, and some of us want different relationships. Some of
us are concerned with meeting our immediate needs and
some of us are concerned with the direction of our lives. In
our discussion, we'll talk about some of the extraordinary
dynamics in relationships and offer you ways to make all relationships easier.

Our premise is that our physical experience is always mirroring the state of our total consciousness. So our sense of
aloneness, our sense of separation, our sense of being under-
loved and lonely, is reflecting to us an opportunity to involve ourselves more with life.

For better or worse, most of us have been influenced by the concept of a never-ending romantic love. This Hollywood-inspired, airport-novel version of life, reflects our desire to be continually in an altered state of consciousness, or literally, or figuratively, drugged. The reality is that drugs wear off and the majority of our life must be spent in the state of consciousness which is unaltered. Dealing with reality is the challenge in relationship.

At the optimal level, whatever it is that needs to be healed in relationship can be healed in the personal relationships we have today. For now, let's put our attention on existing relationships, and a little later, we'll discover how this relates to creating a relationship.

The point is, we need to discover what ideas about relationship we have to the Whole that are being reflected in our relationships to the parts.

As we have already discussed, in the course of our childhood development, events can be interpreted from a childhood perspective that have left us with emotional wounds and scars which need to be healed. The nature of life is wholeness. Healing comes from the old English world *haelon*, which means to make whole. It is innate within nature to return the individual to wholeness. In other words, it is nature's desire that our wounds and hurts and misunderstandings should be resolved, and we should return to wholeness.

I subscribe to the school of thought that natural attraction between individuals is the drug which the universe uses to give us the opportunity to find healing in relationship.

From the medical perspective, the human body naturally creates all sorts of drugs which are spontaneously created in certain situations to promote healing or provide safety; chemicals like interferon and adrenaline. Contemporary writers like Dr. Larry Dossey and Dr. Deepak Chopra have written extensively on the subject.

Whatever the drug is that the body creates when we are stupid in love, it seems to be strong. Not to attack the joy of being stupid in love, but to recognize that relationship is about getting healed, it's not about getting high.

When we were young, if we had strong emotional feelings and were taught by our parent or parents to be more rational, we will most likely attract in relationship a person who is always emotional and filled with feeling, because we suppress that part of our nature. If, as a child, we learned to be needy and weepy, we will probably attract a person who is always demanding that we be logical and rational and make some sense because we overly expressed our emotional nature. In other words, we attract the person who will help us to heal our wounds and resolve our hurts and return us to wholeness.

What often happens in our culture is when that madly-in-love, crazy erotic, joyfully sensual drug of love wears off, we think we must have made the wrong choice or selected the wrong partner. The truth is, when the drug wears off, that's the time

> *Relationship is about getting healed.*

when the deepening of our relationship has the opportunity to truly begin. Nature created romantic love as a powerful healing force in the human condition. Two souls have the power to love one another indefinitely. The larger the love becomes, the more lovable the objects of love become. This is the true foundation of family values.

It is the never-ending quest to personally grow and the willingness to support your partner in his or her own growth that builds the strongest relationships. In order to enter in and to remain in this kind of relationship we must come to the place where we are willing to release the concept that, "the problem with me is you."

When we change relationships without healing the wounds within ourselves, most often we create the same problems in a new relationship. The names are changed, the personalities are different and the problem remains the same. In order to change our experience on the outside, we must change ourselves on the inside.

We must come to the place where we are willing to release the concept that, "the problem with me is you."

The truth is that my problem and my challenges cannot be solved by someone else. I am able to be in relationship as I work on solution, but the solution is not in my relationship with someone else. The solution is in my relationship with myself and my relationship with the whole.

It is impossible to speak about peace without the experience of peace. It is impossible to speak about love without the experience of love. And the same is true of beauty, of harmony, of music and of joy. Yet the mind, unwilling to perceive these qualities, is unable to experience them. The soul, seeking to be in relationship, must begin to discover the qualities that they would seek in relationship, in their immediate experience.

One does not need another person to shift awareness and open the door to possibilities. All of the qualities of life which are birthless and deathless and changeless are immediately available, and the individual must begin to seek peace, love, beauty, harmony, music and joy in the presence of their own existence.

Often this seeking begins in a dialogue with ourselves. It happens that the Universe, or your spiritual nature, is always present wherever you are. So, our self-talk becomes an invitation to the qualities which we seek. Such dialogue might look something like this:

> *"Well, here I am. I exist. My heart beats, my body functions, I think, I perceive, I feel. All of these things that I do are possible because I am. I exist. Whatever it is that I am, I did not create. Somewhere along the course of my life, I discovered it, I became consciously aware of my existence. I am involved in life, and life is involved in me. I must have a relationship to life. Before I became aware of my existence, life was. Before I became aware of beauty, beauty existed. Before I discovered myself in joy, joy existed. Before I ever experienced any moment of harmony, harmony existed. There seems to be a harmonious existence between the earth and the sky, between the planet and the solar system, between the solar system and the galaxy. Harmony, beauty and relationship exist with or without my awareness. These qualities exist in the Universe.*
>
> *The Universe has a relationship with me, and I seek to have a relationship with these qualities. Therefore, I affirm in a new way today that peace, love, beauty*

*and harmony are in my life. I am open to new levels
of understanding. I am receptive to new relationships. I am willing to not only observe, but to also
participate in peace. I am willing to let peace begin
in a new way with me. If my thoughts and attitudes
are creating my experience, I am willing to think
and act and respond in a manner that is life-enhanc-
ing, joy -producing and love-giving. As I experience
these qualities, I notice the people in my life with
these qualities. I begin to make room for deeper levels
of friendship for new friends and new relationships.*

*I am willing to have my hurts healed. I am willing
to express all that I am in wholeness. My ability to
perceive and to think and understand all of this is a
good thing and I am grateful. Since it is the Universe
that is the creative force Itself, I now let the Universe do
Its thing in me, as me and through me. I know it is
good and I say thanks for making it so. And so it is."*

The key to this kind of self-talk is that we make statements
that we agree with, statements which our intellect will not
argue or refute. Yet all of us have a part of our nature which
doubts and which will seek to rebut our new determination
to look at things from an affirmative viewpoint. This is why
it is essential that we arrive at an intellectual understanding
that our optimistic attitude is based on a model of a self-
sustaining, self-enhancing eternity.

The Universe would not be eternal if there were a possibility that a power could operate against It. If the Infinite is
everywhere, then there can be no power against the Infinite
because then there would be two and there would no longer
be an Infinite, there would be two Infinites. Two Infinites

is a mathematical impossibility. So every negation that comes up through our own self-talk or mental treatment of any given situation, can be met with an irrefutable logic drawn from our own mentality. This process of arguing and denying is one of the primary tools in our mental science. The intel-

Our inability to handle our sexuality has led many to seek to ignore it…

lect is insufficient and passion is blind. The Source of passion and intellect must be the only place of reliance. The only place to contact the Source is the self. Hence, a true independence and a real self-reliance is the only solid ground of relationship.

It is wonderful to talk about Spiritual qualities and eternal qualities as the wellspring in relationships. Yet one of the most puzzling and curious aspects of inter-human relationships is sex and sexuality. Often our sexuality is interpreted as either a joke that isn't funny, a riddle that can't be answered, or a flaw in the Divine intention. Our inability to handle our sexuality has led many to seek to ignore it, some who would wish it would go away, and others who seek on the physical level to quell an insatiable appetite.

Walt Whitman said, "If the spirit is blessed and the soul is blessed then the body is blessed." What is so strange about blessing your body? What is so strange about what it actually does? What is so strange about recognizing that your body is sacred?

We have to understand that there is no sin, but a mistake; and no punishment, but the logical consequence of our action. The Universe is actually self-propelling and self-governing, which means it takes care of itself. It knows how to expand each individual soul's awareness. It knows how to take your life as what it really is, which is something of real value, invaluable to Spirit, and guide you through embracing all that you are, to exactly where you are supposed to be.

The greatest mistake of all is to believe that you have either already blown it, or believe that God made some sort of mistake in putting you here, or that some aspect of your being, like your sexuality, was an oversight. As is true with every form of expression, the key to healthy sexuality is to seek to express yourself in that manner which is constructive and life-giving, and therefore harms no one.

Running away from your sexuality is to avoid living your life. Such an action suggests the intelligence of God, or Spirit, or Ralph, the very power that made you and put you where you are, doesn't know what it is doing. To presume that your confusion is smarter than the source of all intelligence is arrogant.

I think the highest respect you can pay to your Creator is to live your life, and live it well…embracing, accepting and honoring everything you are right here and right now, including your sexuality.

Remember our scientist turned mystic, Guy Merchi who said, "All flowers and blossoms apparently without exception, are reproductive organs." Do you think a God that displays sex everywhere throughout all of nature, all over the planet, is against sex? Do you think its against your body? Do you think its against pleasure and sensation? Of course not. And many of us have constricted ourselves, confused ourselves, upset ourselves, blamed ourselves because

Running away from your sexuality is to avoid living your life.

we think we have done wrong, or we think our desires are somehow non-spiritual.

Who shall stand as judge and jury on the sexuality of the world? Dr. Samuel Miller, Dean of the Harvard Divinity School writes about the trial of Joan of Arc. In a moving passage he quotes her as saying, "You say that you are my judge. Take good care of what you do, for in truth I am sent by God, and you are putting yourself in great danger."

As the Universe is self-governing and self-propelling, when you operate against the law, against the nature of the Universe, it will come back and bite. Our sexuality must be expressed against the backdrop of good for me, good for everyone who's affected by it, harms no one and creates a greater degree of livingness.

It is mis-understanding and mis-action that creates pain.

Jack Canfield tells the story of the father of a teenager who, having walked a particular path, comes to a fork in the road. The father points down to his right and advises his teenage son not to go down there. "Down there are snakes and alligators and leaches and quicksand. I've been there, don't go." The teenager says, "Thanks Dad, I'll go see for myself." He didn't know any better. He got stuck. He got bit. He got irritated. He got attacked. Was he being punished, or did he make a mistake? Ernest Holmes was right when he said, "When you truly know better, you will do better."

The Universe doesn't punish. As it is eternal, and birthless and deathless and changeless, it has already built within itself the mechanism to expand itself. Which means there can be no mechanism through which it can destroy itself. When we make a mistake, we pay for it.

When we resolve ourselves to accept our sexuality, and seek with an earnest conviction to express it in a manner that is life-giving, healthy people, places and circumstances will present themselves as a natural expression of an organically-placed libido. Like the flowers, we will be able to stand poised, healthy and radiant, expressing our beauty.

The purpose of every relationship with every individual who is in our lives, is a mutual desire to support each other in our growth. When we expect the other people in our lives, and particularly our intimate relationships, to live in our world, we have placed ourselves at the edge of an ego battle which will inevitably result in conflict.

If we remember that the reason we entered into the relationship was to grow, we will realize that it is never appropriate to surrender ourselves to live in someone else's world. Every relationship consists of three parts; each of the two individuals and the energy that is created by the two together. Each of the parts must be supported and nurtured, comforted and loved in order to feel secure.

In the Aramaic language, the energy of a group is called a *Pagra*. Every relationship has a *pagra*. We remain an individual even though we are part of and connected to various *pagras*. A *pagra* functions much like a joint bank account. Each person on the account must be sure to do their part and contribute. So long as everyone makes a deposit, the withdrawals, by any given member of the *pagra*, don't cause problems.

In relationship we must nurture each individual and the group energy that we create as a relationship.

CHAPTER THIRTEEN

FORGIVENESS

Why do you see the speck in your neighbors eye, but do not notice the log in your own?

Matthew. 7:3

The ideas presented in this book suggest principles which are spiritual. Yet the application of the principles are psychological. Our approach must be to allow an aspect of ourselves which is greater than the ego, or personal self, to keep the wholeness and interrelationship of all things and to allow this perception to operate in our lives.

In recent times, this has led to an advent of a kind of psychology called Transpersonal Psychology. It is believed that this transpersonal self, or Higher Self, is beyond the person in that it can include a greater concept of the whole than can the ego, or personal self. There are, of course, not really two selves. The ego is a reflection of the limited use we are making of the Higher, transpersonal Self. The implications of these concepts are marvelous, because it suggests that wherever we are, whatever pain, confusion, or misalignment we may experience, is but the reflection of the limited use of an unlimited universal idea of ourselves. To the degree that we can expand the concept of ourselves and access this transpersonal aspect of our being, we can change the makeup of our psyche.

The information that the individual receives from the Higher Self is usually experienced as a direct knowing, most commonly understood to be intuition. Our ability to access intuition can be increased by expanding our awareness and acting upon its presence.

The transpersonal nature of the individual is that part of the individual which is able to access intuition, synthesize the individual aspects of the psyche and bring not only the realization of wholeness to the individual, but also an experience of the individual relationship to the whole of life.

The greater our concept of ourselves, the more conscious we are of this super-conscious part of us which knows us and guides us. The more we align with it, the more we experience wholeness. Living in contact with the Highest Self points the way to psychological and spiritual unity.

The Highest Self is always in tune with the Infinite and therefore does not participate in actions or energies which would in any way restrict the free flow of expansive, creative expression (the Universe is always expanding).

At the level of personal self, through our belief in being separate, we have created all kinds of reasons and justifications for stifling the flow of energy and many have gone so far as to redirect the flow of energy from a positive self-expansive force to a negative and destructive force.

Although we are free to act against the flow of our transpersonal nature, such action always results in conflict. The conflict starts in our mind and, if continued, will be demonstrated in our body as disease of one kind or another.

Saints, sages, mystics and philosophers have pointed out the need for forgiveness. Ernest Holmes suggests, "We cannot afford to hold personal animosities, or enmities, against the world or individual members of society. "The reason being, holding any such animosity against anyone or anything serves to diminish the energy in ourselves. In essence, when we hold an anger, a grudge, a resentment, against any person, or anything, to the degree that we are involved in our misdirected energy, we suffer the loss of energy at a level that is exactly equal to our admonishment. In essence, we are making demands and expectations on the Source, others, or ourselves and have agreed with ourselves that unless those demands and expectations are met, we will withhold our energy. It is a curious thing that to the degree you withhold energy, you no longer have that energy.

Ever wonder why on occasion you are so tired?

Dr. Edith Stauffer, in her book *Unconditional Love and Forgiveness,* defines forgiveness as, "the act of canceling the demands and expectations one makes on the Source, others, and the self as a condition for expressing love and other positive attitudes."

This action of cancellation leads to an actual technique of forgiveness which is a way of using the mechanism of the will and the transpersonal nature of the will to correct false belief systems. By means of this process, we are able to work distinctly on several different levels; starting at the physical level, which is the

> *It is a curious thing that to the degree you withhold energy, you no longer have that energy.*

level of the problem, moving through the emotional, where often we feel the problem, then to the mental and finally experiencing the spiritual.

Wisdom has shown simply to be aware of issues and releasing them is not sufficient in our psychological healing. The pattern remains intact and the tendency is to replace one mistake (anger, resentment, etc.) with another. So we seek in the process to contact the transpersonal, Higher Self to activate Its energies—love and wholeness—and allow It to be experienced by the person doing the forgiving. Once the sensation of this energy is experienced, the person doing the forgiving allows the energy to flow out to the person being forgiven.

I was conducting a workshop on forgiveness. Al was separated from his wife for two years. Al had two children age, 9 and 11. The separation had been messy and Al believed his spouse had turned the children against him. Al had a need to forgive his spouse in order that he might begin to live beyond the pain that he was experiencing.

In the exercise we put a chair directly in front of Al and we agreed that he would talk directly to his spouse, Jan, as though she were actually in the chair.

Step One

"Jan, I need to forgive you for…"

Here, Al discovered great rage, deep pain and tremendous anger. He had expected a lot of things from Jan which she could not or did not give him.

Step Two

"I would have preferred that you, Jan…"

The next step was to ask Al to state clearly what he would have preferred. This activates the mind, bringing us out of the emotional level to the mental level where we can creatively begin to make changes. Al's list of preferences was long, involving the inner-most details of their married and family life.

Once he had finished his list, I asked him if there was anything else he would have preferred from Jan. He said he felt complete. I asked Al if Jan had done any of the things he would have preferred. His obvious reply was, "no."

Step Three

"I would have preferred that you, Jan, communicate directly with me, but you didn't do that, and you haven't done that; therefore, I cancel the expectation that you communicate directly with me."

The third step in the process is to cancel each and every preference and expectation. Naturally, simply stating that "I cancel demands and expectations" does not make them go away. It does, however, bring them into the light of our conscious recognition which causes us to realize that they have acted as barriers to our expressing love.

Step Four

"Jan, I now give you total responsibility for your actions, and I take full responsibility for mine."

Often we find that we have taken responsibility for the actions or inactions of another person. It is important then, at this point, that Al give Jan total responsibility for her actions.

Step Five

The next step in the exercise is to access our transpersonal self. As I have previously stated, we are not separate, usually just unaware that at all times, we have the capacity to access our Higher Self.

You are welcome to use this as an example, as a way to access your own Higher Self. Be sure to find a place where you won't be disturbed for the duration.

> *"Al, I would like you to close your eyes and be open to that part of yourself that is at peace, to feel its presence behind all of the turmoil. Be aware of that part of you that loves you now and just as you have always been. Be aware of that part of yourself which knows all about you, that has always comforted and nurtured you and kept you safe. Allow this peace and this wisdom to circulate now through all of your body. Allow it to move into all of those hurt places, all of those tense places, feel it calm you. Allow peace to relax you, allow wisdom to heal you. As you accept this wisdom, this love, this greater truth, you can feel it circulating through your entire body."*

Step Six

> "Al, when you are ready, allow this pure unconditional love to go out from and through you to the chair where Jan is now sitting. When you are ready, send your love out to her just as she is now, and just as she has been. Then say, "Jan, I now release you to your highest good."

As Al relaxed and opened his eyes and finished the exercise, he had new color in his face, his shoulders were more open as though literally, weight had been taken from them. He looked to me with tears of joy and said, "Thank you, I think now I can begin to work with my children."

Al later reported to me that he had been able to work out a custody agreement with Jan and that together, they had agreed not to demean each other to the children. The process of healing and resolving was started.

This forgiveness exercise, which I have outlined through this story, helps the individual to discover where they have hidden angers, fears and resentments in their own psyche. Once we become consciously aware of these issues, we can "cancel" them, making them no longer subconsciously active in our experience.

This exercise is extremely powerful because it works not only on the psychological level, but also at the Transpersonal Spiritual level, thus leading us to a technique which is an applied Spiritual psychology.

It's important to remember that forgiveness is never something you do to somebody else, forgiveness is always something that you do to yourself. It is never wise to shift the energy within yourself and then feel obligated to talk about it with the person you have forgiven. In fact, such action is a doorway to creating further resentments, confusions and angers. Forgiveness comes by canceling the demands and expectations within me which have acted as a condition of my love and other positive energies.

Forgiveness is always something that you do to yourself.

You might discover within yourself a huge list of reasons and justifications that you are right and the other person is wrong. Therefore, the burden of forgiveness does not fall on you, but must fall to them. I remind you, your anger is diminishing YOU.

In our little diagram, Ben is angry at Jerry. Ben believes that Jerry should have performed in a manner that more closely matches expectations. Ben has now decided to withhold his communication, love and friendship until Jerry shapes up. Jerry didn't get emotionally involved in any of this and remains committed to being the best Jerry he can be and allowing his communication, friendship and love to flow.

You will notice that Jerry is just fine and that Ben's attempt to restrict the flow of energy from himself to Jerry, is serving only to block Ben's energy.

It's enough to make ice scream!

The reality is, along the course of our lives, we have stored up with different individuals, different authority figures, different organizations and institutions, all kinds of beliefs that "they" are wrong. There is no one OUT there.

Essentially, we have put trash upon trash to such a degree that simply by removing one stone, which is only a part of the dam that we have created, we cannot instantly open the floodgates to easy living. There is an old Chinese Proverb, "The man who would remove a mountain begins by carrying away small stones." Forgiveness can be an effective and powerful tool in walking the path to easy living. Yet, we must remember, we may have to forgive many and often.

CHAPTER FOURTEEN

BELIEF SYSTEMS

Persistence and determination alone are omnipotent.
                                        Calvin Coolidge

Earlier, we have spoken about affirmations as an effective tool in changing our consciousness. Consciousness changed always results in a transformation which sooner or later shows up in our conscious awareness. Indeed, it becomes manifest in our experience.

Some time ago, I began to repeat the statement "There is always a solution." In the course of our professional lives, our life in relationship, the day to day interaction with technology, challenges present themselves and out of necessity, we are forced to find solution. In the face of such challenges, we have the opportunity to participate in misery, grief, anxiety and stress, or we can watch the magnificence of the Creative Process at work. We can watch unformed substance, energy, or the field of possibilities become specific to our needs, situations and circumstances. The ability to be objective and observe our situations while we are in the midst of participating in them is perhaps one of the most sublime perks of expanded awareness.

Certainly a mere set of words does not constitute a solution. Yet, the repetition of such a specific thought does indeed begin to form a new habit and here is a place of transformation where a set of words becomes an idea actually believed in. And idea believed in becomes experience. To specifically target the exact moment when a set of words becomes a belief is not only difficult but perhaps unnecessary.

In the story of my life, somewhere along the line, it was pointed out to me that in an infinite field of possibilities, solution must always exist. If it didn't exist, it would not be an infinite field, it would be a finite field. My intellectual mind was able to grasp the logic of such an argument, yet, the intellect is insufficient to give us the actual transformative power of belief. So I began to remind myself on a regular basis that indeed, *there is always a solution.* Much like any other affirmation which you repeat, after a while you don't need to think about it, the statement simply moves through your awareness periodically. It certainly is an affirmative thought and therefore it is a healthy habit to acquire much like the affirmation, *I am radiant, vibrant, dynamic, health,* is a good thought to have moving through your consciousness at any given moment. This constant repetition literally creates a *habitual* response of the mind which always seeks to move to the most familiar idea.

It was spring time in the Rocky Mountains. There had been a late snow that season and one of my favorite resorts had stayed open for an additional week to accommodate all the fresh snow. Storms had been moving through the resort throughout the week. Yet, as is true

Certainly a mere set of words does not constitute a solution.

of most circumstances in life, the time had come to move on, in my case, back to California. So I packed up the Volkswagen camper, kids, ski gear, luggage, snacks and drinks for the road, etc. and off we went driving through the peaks of the Rocky Mountains on route to the shores of Southern California. Fifty miles outside of the ski resort, descending from a 12,000 foot peak, a curious red light warning of pending mechanical failure appeared on the dashboard. There being no logical place to stop, my mind jumped to the familiar affirmation, "There is always a solution," and onward we forged. Grabbing the trusty owners manual, we discerned the red light was either referring to the battery or to the alternator. Electrical problems in the middle of nowhere don't seem like a solution. Well, the light wasn't lying and shortly, the engine died on

There is always a solution.

the bottom of a slope, in the middle of a snow storm, on a cliff above the river. Quickly I tried to turn around in a desperate attempt to go twelve miles back to the last town we passed. The engine died in the middle of the turn and we were forced to use the force of gravity to roll back to the side of the road. Reaching for the parking brake and pulling it with some gusto, as there was a cliff, the cable snapped and the parking brake was inoperable. "Oh, shoot, I mean, there is always a solution." Putting the transmission in reverse and releasing the clutch with my foot on the brake, we were safe and I pondered the situation. My wife looked at me and said, "What do we do now?" I responded, "What we need now is help" Just at that moment, a little rented Toyota filled with British tourists came rolling down the hill, stopped, opened their window and said, "Can we help you?" Well, to make a long story short (never one of my strong points), help indeed arrived and we were able to locate the only alternator for a Volkswagen camper to be found anywhere in the Western slopes of Colorado. In short order, we were out of the storm and on the road screaming in delight, "California here we come." There is always a solution.

At some point in the process of my own metamorphosis that simple affirmation had turned into a spontaneous first reflex within my own mind. As a result, circumstances continued to arrange themselves in such a manner that they appeared to match my belief? The entire premise of easy living is that the engaging of higher laws of creation can supersede circumstance and situations and create apparent miracles.

Anything which today seems supernatural, once it is rightly understood, it becomes totally natural.

E.H.

Perhaps you believe that it is self-evident that there is always a solution. Yet I wouldn't be surprised if you have either experienced yourself, or have people in your own experience who's first reaction is panic, not solution. If a simple set of words can actually enter our mentality at such a deep level that they become a belief, then there must be a way to discover and use words that would be appropriate for every area of our life, be it physical, financial, emotions, or mental.

Imagine believing statements such as:

I have an infinite amount of creative ideas flowing through my consciousness.

More and more money is flowing into my life and I deserve it.

I know what I want and I act upon it.

I always make the quality choices.

Everything I do increases my financial worth.

Turning such thoughts into actual beliefs which operate transcendent laws may not be easy, but the path is simple.

It is true: easy living requires persistence and determination.

CHAPTER FIFTEEN

THE BIGGER THAN YOU FACTOR

Look for the good wherever it is and add to it.

The premise of easy living is that you cannot have the Infinite and something else. As soon as you have the Infinite and something else you have more than one Infinite. That's a mathematical impossibility.

The truth is the Infinite doesn't exist everywhere except where it gets to me, stops at me, and then starts again on the other side of me. I'm not an island swimming around in life wondering why I feel isolated. Life must move all the way through you, in fact, the very essence of who and what you are must be life.

I start with a consciousness and out of my consciousness, which is acted upon, something happens in my experience. If life is always responding to the sum total of my consciousness, then why can't I get every thought that I think to become my experience? It is because life responds to what you really mean, not what you think you mean. And because every thought that you think is not in line with the nature of the Universe, nor your own true desires, it does not become experience. Thank God that every thought you think doesn't become reality! So many times, what you think you want and what you truly want are not the same thing.

Each of us has something within us, no matter how deep-seated it may be, that knows we came to experience this life with something to do. We may not know what it is, but it is necessary that we become committed to it and ask questions of our heart and soul every day.

> *I am immersed in the Universe. I am part of the Universe. I belong to the Universe.*

What do you intend to do about the fact that you do not belong to your already used and unsuccessful concepts of yourself? Keep them? Transform them? Come up with something different? Guess what, you belong to the Universe.

We live in a society which has for many years been teaching us not to think, training us to follow the status quo, to accept its limitations, its fears, its doubts, its neurosis and its disease. I'm going to have to pose the bigger questions to myself and be willing to release my tired old concepts if I want to live more in tune with my potential.

Many years ago, the airlines decided it would be much more efficient to take advantage of modern day technology and involve computers to the reservation process. The purpose, to more efficiently serve its customers and streamline technology into the jet age. The airlines then trained their personnel to follow certain protocols in customer relations, which are outlined on the computer screen in front of the employee in the midst of every transaction. I'll tell

Life responds to what you really mean, not what you think you mean.

you a story that illustrates limitation and new ways of looking at what we are given.

Some time ago, my grandfather passed away, and my wife and I had to reroute our travel plans to participate in the memorial service. The day after the memorial, we had reservations to fly out in the morning and my parents had reservations to fly out in the evening. My parents were anxious to return home and asked us if we could switch reservations. In as much as we were in no particular hurry, not to mention their reservations were first class and ours were in coach, I agreed to facilitate the change. I called the airline, explained to them what we wanted to do and made the correct changes with the reservation agent. My parents left on the early flight. Just to make sure things went smoothly, I called the airline again to verify the changes. I was assured that the changes were in place and the reservations were indeed confirmed. We spent a very pleasant day with my relatives on the East Coast.

Just before departing for the airport I decided once again to double check with the airline that things were in place. I was assured all was well and proceeded to the airport. We arrived at the airport and I went to check in. I was promptly told that the flight was sold out and that I did not have a reservation. Directing my frustration to my navel I asked politely to speak to the supervisor. The supervisor proceeded to follow exactly the same protocol that was outlined on the computer for the agent in exactly the same manner and achieved exactly the same result. I regret to report that the anger which I had sought to ground through my navel and into the earth was beginning to bubble over. I explained to the supervisor that he had meticulously executed that exact same protocol as his colleague and that this was not helping to resolve the situation. He explained to me that he was forced to do what the computer told him to do. I explained to him that I had spoken on the phone four times that same day to agents representing his airline and that at no point in any of my dialogues with the airline did I ever speak to a computer. Each of the individuals I spoke with confirmed my reservation.

You may have been in a situation like this in your world. It was, to say the least, frustrating.

Fortunately for me a human being who also worked behind the counter for the same airline had begun to sympathetically respond to the circumstances which led to my frustration. While I was busy arguing that human beings are more important than computers, she had begun to enter my last name with every possible spelling configuration. Just in time to prevent a very non-spiritual, physical violation of the rules of resistance (that which you resist persists and the only thing

Sometimes we have to let go of what we think we want in order to get what we truly want.

that cannot be violated is non-violence), she proclaimed, "I have found it!" I was restored to sanity and courteously placed on the airline in first class as per the confirmed reservation.

The point of the story is that it does not serve us well to be so fixed on our concepts as to lose the intent of our original idea. Businesses use computers to help them to successfully conduct their business. Businesses need people, people need each other. Sometimes we have to let go of what we think we want in order to get what we truly want. It serves us well to focus on our intention and to call forth our intention when we find ourselves meeting any apparent block.

Not long ago, I was negotiating a lease in a nice office building in a nice location and the use that I had for the space was a slight variation of the use-clause that the owner had in his standard lease. The building I was interested in had been built ten years previously and ten years after completion, over 60% of the building was still vacant and had never been occupied.

In our negotiations I asked the owner if it was indeed his intention to own the building and to have it operating as close to full capacity as possible. He informed me that indeed that was his intention. Yet, despite my best efforts to get him to include the possibility of my conducting classes in my own space inside the building, that did not fit his concept of general use for the office building. We were unable to reach an agreement. As a result, I didn't get that new space and his building remained 60% vacant.

Often times in the pathway of our lives, the thing that needs to change is the idea or the tired old concept of how it must be. We need to be willing to change our mind if we are going to change our experience. Sometimes this means letting go of old ideas and accepting a **new thought**.

Indeed Richard Bach announced a powerful Truth;

Argue for your limitations and they are yours.

What is your intention? Can you build your intention? It isn't going to be your every conscious thought that is acted upon, it is going to be the sum total of who you are. Your very beingness is either attracting or repelling something. Are you attracting what you would like to be? If life automatically responds to the sum total of your thought, where are you free? The answer is, *in my thought.*

Thought is not conditioned by time. Thought is not conditioned by space. Thought is free, and I can choose to think what I want to think. My disease, my circumstance, my condition, my challenge is not interrupting the freedom within me to think a new thought. When my consciousness is built to the place where I can respond to the freedom within that new thought, my new thought will become my experience, instantly, magically, or by natural law, all depending on how you look at it.

There is a way for you to constantly live in a world of magic, of good, of light and of truth, where you go from one good to greater good. It is possible and it can happen to you. Do we experience this state of awareness all of the time? Is even the most successful among us experiencing this state of awareness all the time? The answer is, I doubt it. But if we are each day, each moment of our lives, stepping in the right direction, we are on the path to easy living.

CHAPTER SIXTEEN

OUT OF THE BLUE

When answers to a prayer appear in an orderly and unspectacular way, your skeptical friends will tell you it is a coincidence.

Dr. Bill Hornaday

Throughout this book, we have been outlining a mental science which draws its effectiveness from the reality that we live in a spiritual universe which is governed by spiritual, mental and physical laws.

We have established that the Universe responds to our intention. While we are able to prove this in our own experience, by means of demonstrating the principle of which we speak, it is impossible to prove it to the collective consciousness of our society or humanity. Each individual must prove it to themselves.

In our society, when the Universe responds to intention, we call it luck. The consciousness that experiences good fortune isn't lucky at all, it has simply built an attitude of expectancy in some particular arena of their lives.

So perhaps we are at a place where we are willing to call the demonstration of our conviction an act of faith, or perhaps at the very least, we are willing to call it a capital "C," Coincidence... the friend who calls you when you were just thinking of them, the person whom you were talking about, who, later, you *just happened to see* at the market, the carpet cleaner you needed that a friend told you about *out of the blue*, when you weren't even talking about carpets…

I am recommending that to support us on our quest for more comfortable living, we begin to notice these Coincidences and collect them as *lifemarks* along the path of our personal growth and development.

The premise is, thoughts become things. You could say that this happens out of some magical gift of the cosmos. You could also say it happens because it is the law of the Universe. Everything in the physical world, anything that has structure or that we would call form, comes and goes. It integrates and it disintegrates. So if we are measuring our success by the things that we create in our physical world, then we are going to be limited to things and by things in order to know ourselves as successful. Things or experiences are not the measure of success because they will disintegrate and change form. However, if we have success at watching a particular thought become a particular thing, even when the thing is gone, our knowledge of the experience remains. Therefore, creating events, circumstances or things in and of themselves, are not so important; yet the knowledge that we participated in a creative process in order to achieve the success is important. This memory of experience and knowledge is what we get to keep.

> *Notice these Coincidences and collect them as lifemarks along the path of our personal growth and development.*

You see, we are expecting an act of faith to be some big, huge, dynamic demonstration. Yet it is the little acts of faith, building from where we are to where we want to go, that are really important. If you are going to build from where you are, you are going to have to leave something behind to move into a new possibility. To get what you envision for yourself tomorrow, you must leave the consciousness you had today. The consciousness you had today brought you to today,

To get what you envision for yourself tomorrow, you must leave the consciousness you had today.

it will not get you farther than today. Your consciousness is the sum total of everything you have ever thought, said or done. If you want an expanded consciousness, you are going to have to start thinking, saying and doing expanded things.

You are going to need to cooperate with the nature of the Universe. You have to be willing to grow. You have to be willing to get in touch with your true nature. You are going to have to stop going outside of yourself to find authority. You are going to have to sit down, and in the stillness of your own meditation, discover who you are. From this inner place of knowing, you can begin to accomplish great and wonderful things, out of the blue. Because the only blue there is, is the field of amazing consciousness which is waiting for you to embody it. You are immersed in a field of possibilities which will not unfold until you release the old and come in touch with the new. Come in touch with what is possible in your life. Come in touch with the amazing reality and power of the simplicity of a new thought.

Meditation is not so much what you are doing, it is what you are not doing. I'm not doing the dishes, I'm not watching the fly on the window, I am just sitting here and I'm being. In this time of just being, I begin to stretch myself into the dimensionless, timeless, spaceless part of my own being and begin to reveal my Self to my self. The pathway of expanding awareness is expanding our intentions so that the space between our thoughts and our attitudes will be work-

> *Meditation is not so much what you are doing, it is what you are not doing.*

ing for us all of the time. The pathway to easy living is swinging between this inner quest, meditation, and your action, swinging between our dimensionless Self and our active and involved self. This is how we expand our intention.

Most of us have good intentions, but we need to draw them up into our conscious awareness and live our lives in such a manner that we close the gap between what we mean to do and what we do.

One of the great misconceptions in our society today is the concept that *the problem with me is you.* Sooner or later, you are going to have to let go of that idea and take the responsibility that *the only problem with me is what I do not understand.* Understanding is the only real salvation. Life responds to us by corresponding and when we reach into a higher level of our Self, the soul nature of ourselves, we draw a higher level of correspondence and action.

Who I really am is already in tune with the Infinite, is already whole and complete, is already poised and ready, is already creative and productive, is already secure in the knowledge that I cannot give without receiving. Yet my awareness does not serve me well unless I am aware of it. Funny thing about awareness, I discover I have it, then I discover I had it all along, I just wasn't aware of it.

So we have to expand our conscious awareness. It's fair to acknowledge that we have a way to go. But let's start going. Let's take the first step. Let's begin to work today from what we know. Let's begin to explore the possibilities of what can happen when we stand firmly on the conviction of certain truths.

The levels of possibility and the degrees of fulfillment shall be measured out to you entirely in accord with your own measuring. You can only have as much as you are willing to accept at the deepest level of your existence.

CHAPTER SEVENTEEN

KARMA

Joy is the infallible sign of the presence of God
        Teilhard de Chardin

The subheading to any discussion of karma must be the recognition that by whatever name, cause and effect is a Universal law and cannot be ignored. All Universal laws could care little about our argument and care less about our denial of their existence.

The philosopher Ernest Holmes speaks of karma as the *subjective law of tendency set in motion by the individual.* In our earlier discussions we have looked at the concept of a Universal mechanism within what we would call *Mind,* which responds to our deductions. The sum total of those deductions operating at a level beneath our conscious awareness, becomes our subjective tendency. There is a cold, hard, neutral, mechanical nature of ourselves which always feeds back into the experience of ourselves the action of thought we set in motion. Yet, if we allow our knowledge to rest solely on the understanding of laws, whether they are spiritual laws, mental laws, or physical laws, we will find our existence void of texture, depth and color. Certainly any discussion about easy living and karma must include feeling good.

Our understanding of karma must be within the context of the whole. Indeed, our approach is inclusive of an understanding which has been revealed by the saints, sages, mystics and illumined throughout history. While we live in a Universe that is compelled to act in accord with the laws of Its own nature, the very force which impels all of evolution is love. Law without love can be cold and hard. Law, set in motion by self-love, is spontaneous, joyful, alive, creative and filled with an ecstasy that surpasses even our best imagination.

We live in a Universe which is self-propelling and self-governing. The Universe is one big Whole. Everything is inside the circle and nothing can be outside the circle. The way it operates is as a triune unity: Spirit, soul and body. We find this unity within ourselves as conscious mind, subjective mind and effect. Every thought that has ever passed through our conscious mind goes somewhere. This storehouse we have labeled memory. Memory is an active force. While you may not be thinking of any given experience in your life, all of those experiences are right now, in your memory and are right now, having an effect on your life.

Memory is an active force.

For example, take a moment now and think about your high school graduation. If you didn't have a graduation, your mind immediately went back to that age in your life. In your remembering, you remember the way you felt, you remember your best friends, and you can remember even the smallest detail and the feelings within those details simply by being asked for a moment to remember.

Everything you have ever done, everything you have ever experienced, even from the time you were an infant and perhaps before, is in your memory. Therefore, causes you set in motion a long time ago are currently impacting your experience. This is your karma. For many of us, the misinterpretation of events, indeed, the misunderstanding of circumstances, is negatively affecting us today and we are dragging our old karma into our new lives.

Psychology believes that a neurotic thought pattern will repeat itself with a monotonous regularity. A neurotic thought pattern, as far as you and I are concerned, is a negative thought pattern. So now we have a choice. We can get on the couch and figure out what all of our negative thought patterns are or, we can create a new thought. If it is true that neurotic thought patterns will repeat themselves over and over, the implication is that an affirmative thought pattern will do the same.

What is the subjective tendency you are setting in motion? You don't have to look very far to figure out what your own law of karma is doing. Take a look in the mirror. Take a look at your world. What is happening in your experience? What is your perspective of life?

Man will deliver himself from sickness and trouble
in exact proportion to his discovery of himself and his
true relationship to the whole.

Ernest Holmes

You and I will deliver ourselves from sickness and trouble proportionate to our self-understanding. Spiritual laws must be understood if they are to be used for specific purposes. Hidden inside you

We are dragging our old karma into our new lives.

and probably not all that deeply, is a law which is receiving the impress of your thought and acting upon it all the time.

We have been trained to wait for authority outside of ourselves. In the western world we have been trained to use scientific evidence and statistics to support us in our decisions. Perhaps this is the karma of our society. BUT WE ARE FREE TO ESTABLISH A NEW CAUSE TO BELIEVE IN OURSELVES AND OUR OWN POTENTIAL, to follow our own path, to listen to the rhythm of our own hearts, to make our own music, indeed, to sing our own song. We can set a new cause in motion and establish a new subjective tendency which creates a new karma.

Karma is the law of mind. This law can bind you or set you free. It is a blessing and not a burden.

Emerson, the great American original thinker said, "We perceive that we live in a solid Universe but in truth we live in a fluidic universe, that we perceive as a solid fact." The reality is that in truth, everything is fluid because everything is operating in accord with belief, and belief is changing. If I don't like the subjective tendency of my thought, I can change it. It makes no difference whether you think you dragged it from another life or not. If you

It is not about continually reliving your past.

don't like it, you have the power to change it. Easy living is about changing your mind and changing your experience. It is not about continually reliving your past. You are free, right now, to draw from an unlimited field of possibilities, the life of your dreams.

Spiritual activity is what it is, I cannot grasp it, the best I can do is release myself and let it grasp me.
                                                            Joel Goldsmith

When we think about spirituality, we seek to somehow be able to capture an essence, a feeling, a sense which is beyond our words. Yet in this plane of existence, intelligent communication uses words. So it seems that our ability to spiritually advance is going to involve our using words with the Infinite.

Judge Thomas Troward said, "We pray through the articulation of consciousness," meaning that we have to give words to our feelings in order to communicate our awareness. The manifest universe is expanding into infinity, certainly the Spirit of creation must also be infinite. While we may be able to expand forever, we will not absorb the Infinite.

Some of us have areas in our lives that we would like to improve, areas that we would like to enhance. In order to advance, we are going to need to be willing not just to have a distant faith, but come from a platform of self-assertive truth.

God can only know you at the level you know yourself. Easy living can only spontaneously occur in our lives when we are reliant on spiritual power. Many of us are reluctant to give our attention to spiritual reality because we are afraid that we will fail. So we establish within ourselves that we will only try God when everything else fails. Why won't we try God first? Because if we try God and God fails, we will be without hope. So we live our lives holding onto this life preserver: "When everything else fails, I'll try God." Again, we find ourselves posing an interesting dilemma to the Universe.

The Universe seeks that you should know yourself. You are immersed in, surrounded by and part of a spiritual universe. YOU have established the criteria for your spiritual discovery.

Since there is a power that receives the direct impress of our thought and responds by corresponding, what do you think the law will do with your little syllogism, "I'm not going to discover my True Self until everything else fails?" The law responds to this by setting you up so that everything fails. Eventually, you will come to Spirit to be healed and transformed.

It is possible to live your life from inspiration instead of desperation. We must choose to live harmoniously together. We must choose to permit the Universe to use the talents and skills which it bestowed upon us. We must choose to take our hearts with us into the journey of higher consciousness. We must choose the mystical process of affirming and courting the Divine Presence.

Be ye transformed by the renewing of your mind.
Romans 12:2

Transformation is not our department, transformation is accomplished by the natural desire of the Universe to expand itself as you. Transformation is a spiritual process which takes place in the inner planes of your existence. Renewing our mind or making the decision to put our attention on the goodness of life is our department. If you set your wings free to spirit, you will be transformed.

It is possible to live your life from inspiration instead of desperation.

What is self-assertive Truth? Pick any miracle maker you like through history and ask yourself, "How did they initiate or become an instrument through which that apparent miracle took place?" Whether it's the Buddha under the Bodhi tree, or Moses at the Red Sea, or Jesus calling the dead from the grave, it seems these miracle workers were willing to assert the Truth. To us it seems supernatural. Yet if you were to take a pioneer woman out of her time into the present day and turn on the light, you'd scare her to death. It's an interesting concept.

That which today seems supernatural, once it is rightly understood becomes totally natural.

E.H.

Being willing to assert the truth is necessary to bring the experience of our life in tune with our dreams. It is when you know you have a purpose and you assert the truth, "I have a right to live my life and fulfill my purpose," that your purpose will be fulfilled. The assertion of one's own inner knowing appears to be a pathway to revealing truth.

To know God is fun, to have a life without God is anything but fun.

Yogananda

The truth is, there is a field of energy that knows exactly what to do and how to do it. There is an inner knowingness within you that can guide you to the solution of every challenge. We can make the decision to be determined to be healthy, to be inspired, to be enthusiastic and to be prosperous. We will have to stand in our conviction; we will have to assert the truth; and we may have to do it more than once.

Some would say this process is a lot of work. I don't have any magic tricks that would make you free, any coals for you to walk over, or any spoons for you to bend. I do know it is true, if you change your mind, you'll change your experience. The entire process can be fun, joy-filled and life giving.

Make a commitment to have fun, to be joyful, to live your life and to support the spirit within you, and in all creation, and your good will expand. This transformation happens with ease… when you know how.

CHAPTER EIGHTEEN

SIMPLE, BUT NOT WITHOUT EFFORT

*The Universe doesn't care what
you call it, it cares that you call it.*

Indeed, Brownie McGhee's ability to make the guitar sing so sweetly looks easy. We recognize that anyone's ability to master anything did not necessarily come easily. It comes through persistence and dedication. The pathway to easy living is about discovering the nature of reality, and recognizing that reality is an unfoldment of an infinite possibility which is pre-existent. So in truth, making life easier is about our willingness to discover; and then upon discovery, applying a new perception with persistence and dedication.

The guitarist learning the new instrument, learns notes, then chords, then the ability to put chords together. At some magical point in the process of learning, the guitarist is able to make music.

As the understanding of the simplicity of the language of music expands, the music begins to sound more wonderful and to the untrained ear, sounds remarkably complicated. Yet it is the mixing and blending of notes and chords, octaves and harmonies, that create the magnificent symphony of music.

It is also true that the nature of life is, in its essence, simple. There are fundamental principles that operate a self-governing, self-propelling and self-existent Universe. We begin to grasp these principles at the simplest and apparently mundane levels. We seek, at the outset, to take simple thoughts, get clear about them, and discover for ourselves that those thoughts do indeed, become things.

We take the principle of an abundant universe and we apply it at the level that is meaningful to us, where we are today. If the Universe doesn't run out of supply, then maybe I can believe in a parking place, open my eyes, look with a new willingness to receive and find the parking place.

Suppose I have twisted my ankle. I am willing to believe at a new level that it is right and good and life-giving that I should be able to comfortably move, and therefore, I am willing to send, from an unlimited source of love, my personal love and appreciation to my ankle. Perhaps I am willing to discover for myself, that this loving energy in every way

There is a definite correlation between one's attitude of expectation and one's experience.

supports and enhances the natural healing process which is already built into my physiology.

Perhaps I am willing to believe in a new way that everything might, in fact, be interrelated and interconnected, and that my thoughts of love, support and nurturing about my friend, who just lost his job, or my relative who can't shake a bad habit, might actually do some good. If I am clear that the life in her and the life in me is the same life, then my thought about that person, set free, may actually transform itself into a healing and transformative energy that makes a difference.

It is in these little discoveries that we reveal natural law and natural order.

G.K. Chesterton said, "The whole order of things is as outrageous as any miracle which could presume to violate it."

As I gain more and more experience watching these little magic events, I begin to see and prove to myself that there is a definite correlation between thoughts and things. There is a definite correlation between ones attitude about healing and the healing that actually takes place. There is a definite correlation between one's attitude of expectation and one's experience. The tone of the events in my life follow the patterns of my own expectations. As I begin to demonstrate this principle in my experience more consciously, because I have begun to wake up and pay attention to my thinking, I am able to reach a conclusion from the field of my own experience, my life.

If all of this is so simple, and the implications are so profound, why isn't it taught from nursery school up, and why in the world doesn't the media talk about it? Why don't the politicians make reference to it? Why isn't our society leading the way to the world-wide revelation of the power of consciousness? The only answer is that each of us lives our lives for ourselves because we are free and we are given *The only God you will ever know is knocking at the door of your own consciousness...* the ability to make a choice. It is only as each one executes the power of decision for themselves, that the discovery of this remarkable, transcendent and omnipotent authority can be experienced.

Throughout history, the saints, sages, mystics and prophets …the illumined among our forefathers, from Benjamin Franklin and Thomas Jefferson, George Washington to Abe Lincoln, Emerson to Einstein, all have been sharing this truth. Through their inspired lives they have been inviting us to explore the possibilities and begin the quest for ourselves because it is true that only the Self can reveal the Self to the self through the Self. The only God you will ever know is knocking at the door of your own consciousness, waiting to speak to you in a language that you understand and that is meaningful to you.

The Universe does not need our cooperation to function harmoniously for an eternity.

Whether you want to call this an Infinite field of possibilities, Creator, Great Spirit, Ralph, the Originator of the natural order itself, or the movement of natural order, or by any other name, it makes no difference at all! Because Its nature is to respond to what you believe about It, not what you call It. Its manner of responding is always a correspondence. The pathway to easy living suggests that if you expect to experience a greater life on the exterior you are going to have to create the equivalent of that greater life on the inside.

What we are considering, to make our lives easier, is that the building of these equivalents are a mental act based on the understanding that we live in an already existent whole, complete and perfect natural Universe. The nature of this Universe is spiritual. It is absolutely impervious to our arguments against Its existence. The Universe does not need our cooperation to function harmoniously for an eternity.

However, we do need to cooperate with It if we expect to function harmoniously in eternity.

Our pathway to easier living reveals Itself, not through our determination to disprove what cannot be possible, but in truth, begins when we are willing to prove the principles about the relationship between thoughts and experience within the field of our own lives.

We begin by an honest quest to discover what it is that we really want from our lives. It is appropriate to face and solve the challenges in every day existence. It is fair to seek food, clothing and shelter. It is legitimate to meet the demands of income and expenses and taxes. It is reasonable to seek companionship and friendship. It makes sense to fulfill the need to be needed. Yet these things, in and of themselves, do not bring fulfillment.

Heaven is more than a destination. Heaven is a state of awareness where we recognize there is nowhere to go, that the possibilities for good exist now and no matter what my goals dreams and desires are, it is possible for me to live in a contented, heavenly state of awareness now! The challenge and quest of the pathway in consciousness is to bring our mental state, through a persistent and determined elevated state of thought, to a place where the natural laws of the Universe begin to transform our awareness and we feel ourselves living in what appears to be the same world, with a totally new perception. This perception includes feeling and experiencing, recognizing and realizing the texture, depth and color of joy with ever-increasing fulfillment in our daily lives.

It begins with a thought. Thoughts repeated become attitudes. Attitudes are the filter through which we perceive the experience of every external event.

As we build affirmative habit patterns of thought which create within us productive and life giving attitudes, it is the natural power of habit which begins to make our life easier. The mind has an interesting habit, it acquires habits by the repetition of thought.

Once we have habits that support us in building our conviction in the integrity of the Universe, we can begin to expect more than just a little bit of magic. There is not big and small in the mind of the Infinite, there is only the application of principle. Electricity doesn't care whether you use it for a toaster, or a television, a lighthouse or a factory. Since the Universe is the unending source of all energy, it is impossible to diminish it, no matter how much you use. The concepts of big or small and how much or how little, are being measured out entirely through our own mentality. If we are willing to expand our mental equivalent, we can expect an expanded correspondence from the Universe. How much or how little is determined entirely by the individual.

It begins with a thought.

It is wisdom to begin where we are and to begin to move in a direction of our dreams. There is the occasional soul who is so ripe to discover Universal principles that upon seeing the existence of such principles, they are willing to step out in faith and immediately begin to demonstrate profound transformations in their experience.

While we salute such souls we also recognize that where I am is exactly where I need to be. Perhaps the best way for us to begin is to take small steps, clarify our focus, get a handle on our dreams by articulating them to ourselves and start by living from the premise that *I choose to fulfill my dreams.*

Then thoughts, actions and reactions are either moving us in the direction of fulfillment, or they are not. As we begin to become consciously aware of the thoughts, actions and reactions which are not supporting us, we recognize that we can change our mind and begin to think a new thought which will in turn, bring about a new experience.

Thought by thought, experience by experience, we build a stronger foundation and a deeper conviction in the power contained within the unique consciousness that I Am. This new conviction gives us the courage to think more clearly, more affirmatively, more creatively and more productively. Out of my new thought, I am able to observe, in the midst of my own participation with life, the remarkable transcendent authority of amazing consciousness.

As we gain more confidence in the integrity of the Universe, it becomes easier to see that our worries, fears and doubts serve to rob us of the potential joy in any given moment. Such thoughts are also creative, yet they are using the creative energy to move things, conditions and circumstances in the wrong direction. Instead of becoming powerless in circumstance, I can change my mind, create a new perception and begin to work as an effective agent to change my experience for the better.

How much or how little is determined entirely by the individual.

The short form, or easily accessible technique, in catching the negative habit pattern of thought, is to immediately apply an appropriate affirmative thought. The deeper and more transformative approach is to *treat* the situation, circumstance, or negative habit pattern of thought with the

IT'S SO EASY WHEN YOU KNOW HOW

appropriate Spiritual Mind Treatment (see pages 88-89).
This simply involves recognizing the everywhere present
nature of the Universe,
identifying yourself as a re-
creative element in that creative process and through a
process of argument and
denial, bring yourself to the
conclusion that an affirmative thought is more valu-
able than a negative one. You begin to realize and understand that *you* are assigning the value of the things in your
experience.

*You begin to realize
and understand that
you are assigning the
value of the things in
your experience.*

If we have chosen to believe that the reason for our circumstance can be blamed on anyone else, we are essentially
beating a dead horse. You cannot take responsibility for the
actions of anyone else. You can only take responsibility for
yourself. So, if we are hung up in blaming others, we need
to practice forgiveness. This means we must cancel the demands and expectations which are blocking our ability to
love. There is a wonderful saying, *anger is just one little let-
ter away from danger.*

Since you are united, immersed in and surrounded by and
are one with an Infinite field of Intelligence, it is important
that you open the finite to become an inlet for the Infinite.
Clearly, the pathway to easier living demands our discipline
and requires that we take the time to be still and listen to
the wisdom in the silence.

Find a mantra, which can be a word, phrase, or meaningful
concept. Close your eyes and center your attention with
your spine in a vertical position. Repeat the mantra over

and over for at least 15 minutes, every day. The repetition of the mantra moves you into a space which the masters have called meditation. You must be willing to be an effective inlet for Intelligence before you will be an effective outlet for Intelligence.

If you are not sure what to do about situations or circumstances, take the time to be still and ask the infinite wisdom which finds itself centered in you, what to do. Be still and affirm within your own consciousness that the answer exists. Allow yourself to get in touch with the idea that there is always a solution, and invite the Universe to give you a glimpse, to give you a sense, to give you a feel, to give you a thought, or a concept of the solution that you are seeking. Be willing to set aside your thoughts, concepts and ideas and listen to the voice of intuition within you, which always knows the answer. We might call this technique a quest for vision, or even visioning. The name is not important, the Intelligence in action is all important.

You have not been placed on this plane of existence for any other reason than to fulfill your life and purpose. The fulfillment of your purpose is not ordained to be either hard or easy, because the only thing that has been ordained by the Creator for the human experience is our freedom. Freedom is your gift, you may do with it as you please.

We are in agreement that we may as well make it easier, more joy-filled, more loving, more charitable, more prosperous, more enriching and more fun than any experience we have ever had before. Clearly the opportunity to make this life great is the opportunity that is knocking at the doorway of your own existence right now.

I believe that life, filled with joy and happiness, is the easier path. It is the path which can be ours by our willingness to choose it, our persistent determination to demonstrate it in our experience and our willingness to allow life to teach us how, because...

It is so easy *when* you know how.

Will You Live
The Cosmic Adventure?

*Look for the good wherever it is,
and add to it.*

Harry Morgan Moses teaches techniques and practices which support individuals in the discovery of their true nature, illustrating practical, easy to understand methods which empower, motivate and clarify the fulfillment of life goals.

The following items and tape subscriptions are available directly from:

The New Thought Center
8798 Complex Drive, San Diego CA 92123
Phone: 619-974-9830 or 800-417-4004   fax: 619-974-9824

		Qty	Price each
❑	Book: *It's So Easy When You Know How*	____	14.00
❑	Prosperity Power 2-tape (audio) set	____	17.00
❑	Five Tools of Mind 3-tape (audio) set	____	22.00
❑	Seven Steps to Personal Transformation 4-tape (audio) set	____	31.95
❑	Subscription to Tape of the Month.		
	❑ 6 months	____	45.00
	❑ 1 year	____	80.00
❑	I would like more information on available seminars with Dr. Harry Morgan Moses.		

Name _____

Street _____

City/ST/Zip _____

Phone _____

Price includes shipping. California residents add 7.25% tax

❑   Check or Money Order for $ _____

❑   VISA/Mastercard _____ exp: ____

❑   American Express_____ exp: ____